Help Yourself to
Happiness

ABOUT THE AUTHOR

Keith Were has worked for the Australian government and in the tertiary and private sectors as a consultant, lecturer and psychologist. He was a director in the South Australian Education Department and has consulted for the Department of Family and Community Services and WorkCover. He was also a member of the State Registration Board for several years and an associate of Social Options Australia (1995–96). Currently he is an industry consultant. Keith Were has developed and tested this programme for achieving self-fulfilment and happiness for over a decade.

Help Yourself to
Happiness

MIND · BODY · AND SPIRIT·

Keith Were

**GEDDES &
GROSSET**

To Lila (and her guardian angel, Edwina)

This edition published 2007 by Geddes & Grosset,
David Dale House, New Lanark, ML11 9DJ, Scotland
First published in this edition 2004, reprinted 2007

First published in Australia in 1999 by Thomas C. Lothian Pty Ltd

Copyright © Keith Were 1999, 2004

ISBN 978 1 84205 350 8

Printed and bound in Poland
POLSKABOOK

FOREWORD

According to psychological surveys that have mapped human happiness over the last thirty years, we are less happy today than we were twenty or thirty years ago. Paradoxically, our income has more than doubled over that period of time. This certainly leaves us with puzzling questions. What is wellbeing? How is happiness to be attained? In this book, Keith Were attempts to tackle, in a practical way, those very questions. I recommend it to you.

Reverend Tim Costello

ACKNOWLEDGEMENTS

I am grateful to the following for permission to print, or refer to certain previously published material: Simon and Schuster, publishers of *The Five Myths of Television Power* by Douglas Davis; *The Advertiser* (21 August 1997) for information from a survey it commissioned to McGregor Marketing on motherhood.

In addition I am grateful for Associate Professor Leon Earle's personal discussion and permission to refer to his national research work on retired men, *Successful Ageing in Australian Society*, published by Recreation for Older Adults, 1996. Early editorial assistance of the initial manuscript provided by Celia Jellett is gratefully acknowledged, as is the technical assistance provided by Chris Were. I am also grateful for the ideas and support given by colleagues at Social Options Australia, particularly Moira Deslandes.

Finally I want to record the support, interest and encouragement shown by Moira, Tim, Greg, Tess, Bruce and Sandra. Especially have I appreciated the tolerance and encouragement offered by my best friend, partner and wife, Lila.

CONTENTS

INTRODUCTION

This book is about what you want—looking for it, grasping it and holding on to it. It is a guide to travelling the territory of your everyday living and getting the most out of your journey.

- Do you want to feel joyful?
- Are you interested in knowing more about what it means to be happy?
- Have you wondered if you could live in a more contented, relaxed way?
- Does it sometimes seem that you cannot get what you want even though it looks within reach?
- Are you ever unclear about what you want?
- Do you feel dissatisfied even when you achieve your goals?
- Do you think there is too much excitement in your life, or perhaps not enough?
- Do you want to know more about what you can do, and what you can use, to help yourself become happier?
- Do you have difficulty in finding the way back to a happy frame of mind after you have become unhappy?

If you have answered 'yes' to these questions then this book may help you.

Knowing where you are going
(to find happiness)

Your first objective is to be clear about what you are seeking and where you are going. This means you will need to think and plan! At work, in order to encourage planning, a team leader often says something like: 'If you don't know where you are going, then you are not likely to get anywhere.' This is also true for you.

You may think you know what will make you happy, but when you take the appropriate actions to achieve your goals you do not get what you had hoped for—the results of your efforts do not match your expectations. This could be because what you were aiming for was not the right target, or because you did not use the right means to get there. You probably recognise, for example, the truth of the old saying that 'money cannot buy you happiness' yet many of us seem to pursue it for all we're worth. The problem is that the saying is only half true. More money will buy you some of the extra comforts of living, but it will not make you satisfied with your work, yourself or your partner.

This book explores your views on happiness:

- What are they?
- Where did you learn them?
- How true are they?
- Does the reality of your expectations live up to its promise?
- What actions can you take to obtain happiness?
- What actions should you avoid?

For you to acquire and hold on to happiness, it is important that you clearly understand your own views on it. This is because most of what you do stems from what you believe and think. Even when you are urged to act by your biological feelings (for sex, food and physical comfort) your actions are often moulded by your thoughts and beliefs (about how you should behave, about religion, about the law, or about the likely success of your actions). You may restrain yourself from overeating, for example, because you believe that it is wrong to be self-indulgent, or because you think that eating particular foods will make you sick, or fat.

Beliefs, views and thoughts play a central role in what you end up doing. Some people have such strong beliefs they are prepared to die for them.

You need to be able to sort out the beliefs, views and thoughts that accurately show you the way to wellbeing and happiness, and separate these from the half-truths, mixed messages and wrong ideas that lead you in the opposite direction. You also need to work out the best path to follow to achieve the right goals—the ones that will make you happy.

What this book is—and is not

Happiness is found in the ways you react to the variety of life's experiences. There are many books, tapes and spiritual gurus that seek to tell you what to do to be happy. The difficulty is that life is as varied as the ways you can think and feel about it—single-focus approaches rarely cover the territory.

You need to be able to find or regain happiness in your everyday life—washing the clothes, painting a fence, managing a promotion, or coping after the loss of a loved one, as well as in the more commonly recognised and more loudly proclaimed requirements for happiness, such as effective relationships and personal achievement. This book has been written with the whole gamut of life's experiences in mind.

Help Yourself to Happiness asks you to examine what you think is important in living, and, in this sense, the book is about social, moral, and spiritual issues. It contains suggestions and strategies to use to bring your daily living more in tune with what you want and what you think is important, and in this sense it is a self-help book.

This book is not for the passive reader. Although there are suggestions which you would be likely to be given in a supportive professional context, like possible ways of sleeping, thinking or acting more effectively, it is not just a book to be read, it is about doing things to get more out of your life.

How this book is arranged

Part 1 looks at what is meant by happiness and what kind of happiness you want. Part 2 covers the eight principles of happiness and how you can apply them in your life. The final part of the book looks at ways in which you might move forward.

Three kinds of activities are specifically provided:

- Exercises are given to help you learn a particular idea or skill.
- Points for reflection (and examples) are generally used to illustrate a point.
- Tips are given on managing life circumstances.

Real-life stories taken from my work and the experience of others are included to show how happiness principles can be applied. Circumstances and names have been changed in these stories to provide anonymity.

How to use this book

While the book has been set out in a sequence which takes you from identifying your goals to learning how to reach them, you may find there are parts you want to spend more time on than others. For most people, however, following the chapters in order and doing the exercises is likely to lead to the best results. It is something for you to enjoy working on. Go to it!

PART 1

LEARNING ABOUT HAPPINESS

Happiness is . . .

'Happiness is a sad song' (*Australian Magazine* 1995)
'Happiness is a computer boom' (*Bulletin* 1983)
'Happiness is a positive cash flow' (*Rydges* 1983)
'Happiness is a warm gun' (*Juice* 1995, John Lennon)

Happiness means different things to different people—nothing is more certain than that! Although it is possible to look at happiness in many different ways, two simple points stand out. You can have *goals*, and you can use various *means* to reach them. When we think about happiness most of us think about our goals—health, wealth, power, pleasure, or success.

Let's examine three categories which can be used to describe our happiness goals.

Defining happiness

Goals
I use three key words to define happiness goals:

- the *comfort* goal—means seeking good health, an absence of pain and the full range of sensual pleasures.

- the *control* goal—is about the extent to which power, influence, freedom, control and status figure in your state of happiness.
- the *creativity* goal—includes those aspects of your life where you gain happiness through creativity, development and productivity.

In this book, *comfort*, *control* and *creativity* are used as a shorthand way of referring to the goals of happiness. In the next chapter, there are exercises which help you sift through the myriad decisions you make every day, and look at them in terms of your comfort, control and creativity goals.

There can be overlaps between these goals. An architect who designs a building, for example, will include elements of *comfort* as well as *creativity*. A special case of overlap between *control* and the developmental aspects of *creativity* is shown when you are able to influence others by your charity and compassion.

Means

How you go about achieving your goals is both a moral and practical matter. It is a moral matter in the sense that what you *do* to obtain happiness can be 'right' or 'wrong'. It is also a practical matter because being happy depends on your actions.

I might, for example, want the reasonable goal of increased family income (and the resulting increased *comfort*) and believe I have the skills to cheat on my tax return. To exercise these skills, however, I may need to compromise my values, which would cause me to feel distressed. In this case, choosing the wrong *means* to increase my income can be the cause of unhappiness. To pick another obvious example, it is hardly good for other people if I gain excitement or pleasure from causing physical pain to others. Such 'immoral' goals are not likely to bring me long-term happiness.

Happiness comes from having suitable goals *and* using suitable means to achieve them.

Knowing where and how you learnt your views on happiness can help you to accept them, or try to change them. It can prepare you to answer questions like:

- Is what you appear to value really what you want?
- Are the means you are using to achieve happiness likely to be successful?
- Can you change what you want, how you go about getting it, or how you feel about what you already have? (Some of us seem happy with very little, others never seem satisfied!)

Who taught you about happiness?

Parents and peers

Other people are a key source of what you have learnt to think is important. As a child you would have learnt from your parents and friends in an informal setting. When you were a teenager, your peers became even more important 'teachers'.

What your parents and peers have taught you depends on their culture. Everything that you learn through the culture of schooling, games, sport, music, films, radio, television and newspapers, if you live on the banks of the River Ganges, in India, is going to be different from what you would learn if you live on the banks of the River Thames in London. Some of these differences are becoming less noticeable. As international communication through commerce, film, television, print and the Internet becomes more advanced, the values and ideas of countries, such as the USA, that rate high in communication are more likely to be transmitted to other countries of the world. It seems you can go just about anywhere in the world and pick up American CNN television. Conversely, the views and ideas of smaller groups may struggle not to be submerged in their own country's mainstream values, recreation and customs.

You can change your views by contact with other cultures. You may also acquire knowledge, new ideas and fashions from parents, peers and other teachers.

It is common for older members of a group to express concern about the behaviour and attitudes of the next generation: 'We didn't behave like that in our day'. There are also attitudes and views which tend to persist in groups over generations, for example: an Irish sense of humour, and a French attitude to wine.

Clearly not all you have learnt to value as important and likely to make you happy comes from your parents, friends or cultural background. Some of it comes from your own questioning—you are not a mere replica of your parents and friends. In the same way, your acceptance or rejection of scientific and religious views adds to your values and so contributes to your personal description of what you want. Your friends and workplace mates can often be influential in this process. Adopting their views can gain you acceptance and you may find that the new view or idea appeals to you.

Your views might also have been influenced by teachers at primary and secondary schools, in post secondary school training, and by teachers in the media.

Teachers

Your parents and peers have themselves been substantially influenced by their own teachers and the extent of their exposure to and absorption of community and media messages. An advertisement describes the thrills you will get from driving such-and-such a car, a magazine article trumpets the great joys to be experienced from using shower gels (theirs of course), a television series 'tells' you how to behave if you want to be rich and famous. Are you persuaded by any of these happiness packages?

The message reflects the learning of the messenger. Even articles describing actual events send messages expressing the views of the writer. However, what journalists believe may sometimes be false.

FOR EXAMPLE

Let us suppose a reporter wrote: 'Unable to suppress his desires, Billy Jones, paedophile, was constantly on the prowl around schools looking for new victims.' The assumption is that Billy Jones has uncontrollable urges. This may be a false assumption—the urges may be controllable—but the view of this imaginary journalist could influence us to have a mistaken or at least incomplete understanding of how sexual needs work.

Moreover, those who write for the media are rarely free agents. A journalist's idea can end up on the editor's cutting floor, never to be seen in print. Similarly, what you eventually see on your television news is the work of a group of people, some of whom have more say than others.

The powerbrokers of the media in all its forms are the modern day town-criers. They are not immune to the influence of ideas they have learnt. These ideas may include inaccurate, poor, or misunderstood science, as in the example above. The town-criers' ideas influence what productions, articles or films are approved or what changes are made to them. In a way this material is censored.

Town-criers not only promote their views by omission, but also in the way news is presented: the headline; the size of the print; the location of the information (a news item seems less important if it is the last few lines on page 20); and by the kind of mood music, style or format used for a television or film presentation.

The powerbrokers of the media in all its forms are the modern day town-criers. They are not immune to the influence of ideas they have learnt.

Some members of the media are consciously biased, others strive for objectivity, and yet others attempt to reflect what they think we *want* to be told, see or hear. They can be wrong. They can also be completely unaware of how their personal background shapes a story.

How did you learn about happiness?

Learning by example

Most parenting books advise parents to teach by example. It is certainly usual to find that children raised in sporting families see sport as a major source of enjoyment, either as participants or as spectators, that children growing up in families where there is music see music as an important source of pleasure and, similarly, that children brought up by curry eaters are likely to favour spicy cuisine! While individuals may reject one or more of their family values and also acquire new ones as they grow up, it is also rare for children who, say, experience little music in their lives to become musicians as adults though, of course, it does happen sometimes.

Having examples and models in your life, whether in your family or outside it, are clearly ways by which you have learnt what you think will make you happy. You are likely to be influenced to behave as your models do because you admire them, or you may go in the opposite direction if you believe their behaviour is wrong; for instance, a son of a drunken father may become a teetotaller.

Learning through rewards

The most obvious way that parents teach their children about desirable values is the 'carrot and stick' principle. You come to see those actions for which you are rewarded as necessary for your happiness. Thus you learn to play cards, to go fishing, to be polite, to be friendly, to work hard, to be quiet, or to love food. Of course, to be effective, the rewards need to be meaningful. Although rewards like praise are commonly effective, in some circumstances money, food, or presents are used to recognise 'good' behaviour. Sometimes an absence of criticism can itself encourage you (as a child or adult) to continue the behaviour that produced this result. You could call this the *it's-beautiful-when-it-stops* factor, which comes into play for example, when you stop criticism from others by taking your muddy shoes off before you come inside, or by turning down the loud music, or by arriving home on time.

Sometimes 'carrots' are given in a step-by-step way. Not only do you learn to value a particular behaviour, say, saving money as a means of obtaining future comforts, but you may also learn the way to do this. Thus some children are first encouraged not to lose the money they have in their hand while they are on the way to the shop, and then later to put money into a school bank account, and then to save for a new bike and so on.

Learning through stories
One of the main strategies that adults use to impart values, attitudes and behaviour to their children and to each other, is by telling stories and using little sayings.

FOR EXAMPLE
Some common examples of learning through stories are given below.

• To teach you to be friendly or that acting 'normally' is important, an adult will say to a child pulling an ugly face, 'Your face will stay like that if the wind changes.'

• To teach you that buying something cheaply may actually cause you to pay more money in the long run, you might be told to avoid being 'a penny-wise and a pound-foolish'. As well as saying that it is a good thing to spend wisely, this saying also suggests, incidentally, that money is important.

• The story of 'the tortoise and the hare' has often been used to teach children that persisting, even in the face of difficulties, is a good idea.

- Some stories teach something different from the message the storyteller intended. Stories of ghosts, bogeymen and unpleasant relatives, for example, have been used to frighten children into being obedient. Instead what may be learnt is to be afraid of imaginary situations.

Learning what is important through your body

Basic biological needs also teach you that some matters are important. Thus most of us, in one way or another, think food, drink, sex, shelter and the absence of pain (which includes health) are important. It is also true that your beliefs, ideas and values may colour your attitude to these aspects of living. So how you satisfy these wants will vary with the ideas you have learnt about them. Whether, for example, you drink Coca-Cola®, Scotch whisky, beer, tea, coffee and full cream milk, reduced fat or soy milk, or all of the above, depends on what you think will make you happiest (and not just for their short-term effects!). These are choices you have learnt from your 'teachers' (parents, peers, school teachers and town-criers).

There is also a view that desire for respect, status, companionship and love at least partly comes from your biological make-up—the way your human body and brain works—your 'hard wiring'. Studies of some animals suggest that actions used to acquire status and gain control of a group of fellow animals may be, in part, instinctual. Even if this is partly true, it is clear you also need to *learn* how best to achieve (or not to achieve) status, respect and love. How you understand them is influenced by your childhood and teenage years and the teachings of your life experiences.

How you satisfy your need for food, drink, sex, shelter and the abscence of pain varies with the ideas you have learnt about these needs.

In the same way that you form a view about eating and drinking, even your curiosity, creativity, your aesthetic and pleasure-of-knowledge goals appear to be a mixture of biological and social learning. In this analysis, your urge to investigate, discover and create are seen as a natural part of you, though what you choose to do in this way depends on your learning. Imagine that at some stage during your life you want to draw something; whether you use ochre colours on bark, a pencil on paper, or a computer program such as 'Paintbrush' will depend on your background and learning.

Further removed from direct 'teaching' by your body, but perhaps influenced by it, are ideas that you have learnt about how charity, compassion and acceptance of others influences your happiness.

Learning from the media
Television, films, books and newspapers make use of most of the teaching methods described above. They use parent figures and peers; they use punishment and rewards; they express views about sexual behaviour.

Learning overall
Not only have you learnt some of your happiness goals in the ways discussed above, but equally importantly you have also learnt to select certain methods, strategies or practices to obtain them. How you use rewards, stories or follow examples to help you get what you want is something you have learnt. Even when, for example, you do not learn what the person criticising you is trying to teach you, you may have learnt to use criticism as a teaching method.

As your first step in helping yourself to happiness you can check on how you have learnt your happiness goals and what some of them are. I suggest that you do the checklist provided on page 26 and keep the results for later review. There are no right or wrong answers. It is an exercise to help you recognise how you learnt what you think will make you happy.

Exercise 1: Learning happiness checklist

As a child:

1. Praise

Name two examples of behaviour that earned you praise. Examples: being neat, helping others, being quiet.

_____

_____

How were you praised? Examples: given sweets, told how good you were, bought a toy.

_____

_____

2. Punishment/criticism

What were you punished/criticised for? Examples: told off for throwing stones, eating too much, hitting your brother or sister.

_____

_____

How were you punished/criticised? Examples: hit, growled at, sat in a corner.

_____

_____

3. Other forms of encouragement/rewards

What were you given? Examples: money, sweets, outings.

_____

_____

What were you encouraged to do? Examples: read, learn self-defence, how to fish, sew or do sums.

_____

_____

4. Learning by example

Name three or four adults that you admired. Examples: father, mother, aunt, a significant adult such as a pastor, priest, sportsperson.

PERSON A _____

PERSON B _____

PERSON C _____

PERSON D _____

What did they do that you admired?

PERSON A _____

_____

PERSON B _____

_____

PERSON C _____

_____

PERSON D _____

_____

5. Sayings

Name a saying that impressed you. Example: Rome wasn't built in a day.

_____

_____

What did you learn from it?

_____

_____

6. Stories

Name a story that has influenced you. Example: Snow White.

_____

What did you learn from it? Example: good triumphs over evil.

_____

_____

Note: In this section some of the teachings you remember may have been direct, for example: 'Eat your crusts and you will grow nice curly hair', and some may have been indirect. Perhaps you saw your mother do everything for your father and you decide that you're never going to do that.

Please remember that sometimes the 'teacher' may have been a character from a film, a television show, or an article in a magazine, or a hero/heroine in a book. This could even apply to the previous questions as well as the ones below.

7. Food

What were you taught about eating? Examples: how much food, what kind of food, a dessert is for being good, think of all the starving children and don't waste food.

_____

_____

Who taught you? Examples: parents, school, friends.

_____

_____

How did they do that? Examples: through little stories, rewards.

_____

_____

8. Alcohol

What were you taught about alcohol? Examples: when you are an adult you can drink (i.e. drinking alcohol means you are an adult), no one should drink because it poisons your brain.

_____

_____

Who taught you? Examples: parents, other family members, peers.

_____

_____

How did they do that? Examples: stories, sayings, rewards.

_____

_____

9. Pain

What were you taught about coping with pain? Examples: you must take something to get rid of it, do not cry or be a baby.

_____

_____

Who taught you? Examples: parents, friends, relatives.

_____

_____

How did they do that? Examples: by telling stories about how their pain

had gone away when they took medicine, by giving you a sweet when
you didn't complain.

_____

_____

10. Health

What were you taught about how to keep healthy? Examples: taught to
brush your teeth, told stories about germs, or about the need to go to bed.

_____

_____

Who taught you? Examples: parents, other adults, other children.

_____

_____

How did they do that? Examples: by telling stories about getting sick, by
punishment or rewards.

_____

_____

_____

What do your results tell you?

Your answers will reveal some of the major influences on the
way you live to obtain happiness. It is important to realise that
you will probably have learnt some attitudes and views which,
despite the best intentions of your teachers, act contrary to
your happiness if you use them. If, for example, you were
rewarded for your 'good' behaviour with food, you may have
learnt a form of short-term happiness, overeating, that is contrary to your long-term health and happiness.

You *may* even have learnt to desire unpleasant experiences. It is sometimes said that children who receive attention mainly through criticism seek out criticism because they have learnt that they are recognised by it (and to be recognised is highly desirable, even when the recognition comes in an unpleasant form). It may be that, for some of us, unpleasant treatment is more pleasant than no attention at all, even though this may lead to long-term unhappiness.

There may also be characteristic ways of behaving that the person feels will give them more satisfaction, attention and recognition. My grandfather, a Scot, used to say, 'A Scotsman is never happy unless he is miserable.' While I know this is not true for Scots in general, it was sometimes true of my grandfather!

Among the views that you have learnt will, of course, be ones that have worked for you. They will be goals that you find you know how to achieve and which give you satisfaction and happiness.

In addition to the goals that you have learnt to believe give you happiness, you perhaps have also learnt the means to achieve them. This often is about how you treat others. To reach your goals, you may seek to influence, manipulate and control others to get them to do what you think will give you more happiness.

Your answers to the kinds of ways you were praised, rewarded, criticised and punished and the kind of behaviour you saw and thought was successful for others can be the kinds of methods you favour.

REFLECTION

Go back to Exercise 1 (page 26) and consider which happiness goals you have learnt and still use—about health, pain, forms of reward or punishment, or stories that still impress and influence you. What did you learn that you echo in your relations with your friends, partner or children?

A special teacher

One of your teachers, the media, often reinforces the views you have already learnt from others. The methods of instruction are the same as the ones used by your other teachers. So, to discover what a particular television, film or newspaper item is trying to teach you, ask yourself: Who gets rewarded? Who gets punished? What kinds of rewards and punishments are used? Which role models are portrayed favourably? Which biological appetites are supported and in what way? Which ones are discouraged? Which strategies for getting what we want are shown to be successful?

Naturally, you will not of course have agreed with or absorbed everything the media has told you. Even from your childhood days you may have rejected, avoided or not listened to ways of getting happiness that were contrary to your own. In contrast you may have sought out and embraced ideas and heroes/heroines that endorsed your own views—a practice most of us have used.

In addition, magazine articles, television shows and films will present different, sometimes even conflicting views.

FOR EXAMPLE

Perhaps you have just read an article on how terrible anorexia is and how its origins in part relate to placing undue importance on appearance, then on the next page you read an article on the success of a beautiful and slim model, or how Elle McPherson needs to avoid getting cellulite on her bottom!

Despite sometimes conflicting opinions and your own selectivity with respect to media programmes and purchases, prevailing views portrayed in the media support certain values and ways of behaving. Some of these may lead to increased personal happiness and some may not.

The power of the media to influence behaviour has been well recognised by contemporary governments, totalitarian regimes and dictatorships. During World War I, there were well-documented campaigns to encourage young men to volunteer and to participate in battle. The Nazis in World War II even had a ministry of propaganda. The control of media, in today's democracies, continues to be a controversial matter. There is little doubt that the media plays a substantial role in maintaining and establishing the views you have on how to acquire and hold on to happiness.

Summary

You have learnt that:

- you have views on the sort of *comfort*, *control* and *creativity* which will bring you happiness.
- these views on happiness have been formed by your teachers, that is, your parents, friends and schoolteachers, your own body and the media, referred to as town-criers (which includes magazines, newspapers, television, film, radio and books).
- the means by which you have learnt these views have included learning by example, through rewards, criticism, stories and the messages your body gives you.
- the media supports and adds to the views you have learnt from your other teachers.
- the means you are likely to choose in your pursuit of happiness are also likely to be ones by which you were most influenced.

The next step is to look at the particular happiness goals you have learnt, including some which are represented on film and television.

YOUR HAPPINESS GOALS

Foremost among your teachers are your parents, friends and workmates. Much of what the media tells you is a reflection of what you have already learnt from them. Thus the media can give you an indication of what, perhaps, you already believe is important, as well as being itself a source of influence.

This chapter looks first at the media's support for and influence on your views of happiness, and then at your personal happiness goals.

Special attention is given to misleading views, as these are the ones that need to change if you are to achieve long-term happiness.

Ratings for happiness

Ratings for film and television and the circulation figures for magazines and newspapers receive considerable attention because they are an indication of present and prospective income. Ratings can also be indicators of the extent of your absorption of, or agreement with, the popular views of happiness as portrayed by the media. Of course, if you are like most of us, you will also occasionally watch programmes with which you disagree.

As an exercise, go and look at an entertainment ratings table. They can usually be found in the weekend newspapers, or you could do a search on the Internet. Now examine the top ten films and what do you find? The top most-watched films are usually excitement vehicles. They are films about experiences that are outside the realms of everyday living. There are 'good guys and bad guys' movies where strength, skill and aggression are rewarded and frequently a social comedy where the lead tries to find happiness and love but is forever hopelessly off the track. Analyse the content of blockbuster films. Do they have a plot which has elements in the following areas?

- Retribution is favoured as a means of dealing with the unsavoury—making sure the villain gets his come-uppance—based on the principle of 'don't get angry, get even'.
- Violence is shown as a way of reaching a goal; often this is shown through historical events where the violence is sometimes successful and sometimes unsuccessful. There is a strong element of the 'underdog having his day' in this type of film.
- There is a heavy emphasis on relationships and how to behave in them.

The most-watched television programmes are usually soaps, such as *EastEnders*, and programmes that cover topics such as news, health and lifestyle, comedy and sport.

Making sense of visual entertainment

Whether films and television programmes strengthen your opinion or lead it in different directions, they indicate goals and procedures you may favour to achieve or increase your happiness. Some attitudes and actions depicted by the media are obviously useful for improving short- and long-term happiness. Ideas such as:

- Forgiving friends their shortcomings (often in soaps but also in film).
- Making sure you understand what is said or meant before proceeding (the negative consequences of not doing this are often seen in comedies).
- Excitement which keeps your adrenalin and other hormones flowing—the benefits may vary according to your state of health!
- Seeing effective ways of relating to others; sometimes ineffective ways may also show you what not to do.
- Encouraging your development (gardening, home improvement), stimulating your thinking, curiosity, creativity and aesthetic appreciation (news, documentaries, exploration and travel, arts and science programmes).

In addition to its other uses, visual entertainment shows some trends that may or may not help. It depends. Some may reflect your current thinking; some you may enjoy but not take too much to heart; some you may think you are not being influenced by but are; some you may recognise as being not useful to your long-term happiness but watch anyway; and some you may avoid.

Half-truths and mixed messages

Success comes from being ruthless
Direct attack methods may sometimes succeed in business and some sports, including most football codes, but certainly they do not always work, and indeed there is an increasing range of professional opinion that says this. Additionally the process may seriously hamper your equanimity if it conflicts with your fundamental values.

Happiness comes from emulating your heroes

It may but, again, to do something you believe is wrong won't bring you happiness.

Good luck, magic and angels will help you out when you need it

This probably comes into the category you may not believe but sometimes use—it is only a problem if it leads you in unhappiness directions (e.g. gambling to excess) or prevents you from attempting to find solutions to your problems.

The world is made up of good guys and bad guys (and never the twain shall meet)

A view that can lead you down the track of payback, revenge and frustration and away from development, change, improvement and rehabilitation.

Violence can solve your problems

It doesn't work.

You have to be thin to be attractive

This is absolutely not true! A smile, a laugh, a twinkling eye is often the most attractive thing about a person apart from personality! Furthermore, the thin supermodels and the hunky male models are an advertising strategy which goes like this: if you buy my product, you buy my glamour.

You need a girlfriend/boyfriend to be happy

Again, this is plainly not true. Happiness is not an equation like this.

The list above doesn't cover everything. Why don't you try to add a few more messages you may have identified? Are they true messages or misleading?

Written media is dominated by daily newspapers and magazines which have increased in variety and quantity since the days when the *Women's Weekly* was the main fare for most homes, as a stroll today down the aisle of any newsagent will easily demonstrate. These influences have become part of our everyday lives and should be viewed in the same light as films and television.

REFLECTION

Consider the media's support for and influence on your views of happiness.

- At this stage, you may find it helpful to recall the names of, say, your two favourite films (including videos) and ask yourself what you liked about them. What messages did they give that you think would support your long-term happiness? What messages were suggested that you think would detract from your long-term happiness?
- Now think about the last magazine article you read. What was it trying to teach you?

Doing what you are told

A common approach to journalism seems to be to provide information from surveys of public or expert opinion on children, on music, on television, on sex, on anything—hardly a day goes by without a newspaper reporting an opinion poll. Changing views on government and opposition parties are regularly solicited. Similarly most magazines and many television current affairs programmes tell you what views are most popular. Key public figures and retiring dignitaries are sometimes used in a similar way to tell you what you should be thinking, or what you will be thinking if you aren't already!

Fortunately, we are mostly able to use our discretion in what we absorb. Nonetheless you may sometimes change your opinion and your behaviour, or be supported in your resolve to follow a particular path by what you read and hear—which is only okay if the survey results or expert opinion are correct.

FOR EXAMPLE

For a number of years since the 1950s we have been told different stories about child-rearing. One simple but concrete example
is how to feed babies. Should it be done on demand or at particular times? Is formula milk or cow's milk best for a child's health?
How important is it to breastfeed? One recent study reported the
positive effects of breastfeeding on the development of intelligence. Yet views on best practices change with different surveys,
opinions and analyses. What are we to believe?

Parents must wonder what they have to do to get it 'right' and
sometimes they may end up feeling guilty because they have
not followed the 'correct' advice. Not a good thing for happiness. Resolving the wrangles of professional opinions can be
done by using balanced judgement. If an 'expert' says everyone should behave a certain way, be wary. While all children
may need to be immunised, it is far less clear if all children
should be breastfed—it depends on the child, the feelings and
health of the mother, and other family circumstances. Pre-
scriptions on how parents should raise their offspring are
even less likely to be universally appropriate.

More recent opinion polls continue to tell us how to feel,
think and behave. One such survey commissioned by *The
Advertiser* (21 August 1997) and conducted by McGregor
Marketing was based on what women thought was most
important. The headlines of the day implied that women
wanted motherhood and power. Detailed results said that:

- while motherhood (bringing up children) was highly
  ranked, being a wife or partner wasn't; also lowly ranked
  were home duties, career and sex.
- highly rated, in the following order, were: financial independence, traditional family values, different body
  shapes, more power in politics and in business, and a
  fairer deal in the workplace.

Survey messages can be mixed. In this survey women gave a high value to motherhood and financial independence, while a wife and partner role was rated lower. This could be seen to suggest single parenting. Yet in the same survey, family values (which in commonsense language implies a partner) are rated highly and careers (a major source of financial independence) are rated low. Confused?

Politicians are often wary of public opinion surveys. One reason for this is that there is a strong suspicion that the survey results themselves can sway public opinion. If the trend is shown to be going in a certain direction, the fear is that some people not surveyed may change their future vote perhaps in the direction of the reported trend. It seems likely that published survey results themselves may change some people's opinion of an issue.

So, you have seen that there are a number of messages your teachers are sending you; sometimes helpful, and sometimes conflicting. Remember, what you think is what matters.

Your happiness goals

The exercise below is designed to clarify what you think is important at this point in time.

Exercise 2: What is important to you?

1. Comfort

Most of us engage in many *comfort* activities every day. Place in order of importance to you the seven *comfort* goals and associated activities listed below. Placing food seventh, say, does not mean you intend to stop eating, only that you prefer other goals and activities before eating. Indeed if you happened to be anorexic you may place food first, not because you are eating frequently, but because eating and its avoidance would be very important to you.

Place the following *comfort* goals in order of importance:

- food—includes eating out, having strong food preferences, preparing food, wanting food promptly when you are hungry.
- health—includes exercise, dieting for health reasons, healthy lifestyle, illness prevention and treatment.
- pain—includes desire to avoid pain, using painkillers.
- sex—includes sexual activity, following or paying attention to media programmes with a strong sexual focus (e.g. the film *Basic Instinct*, 'how to' articles in magazines and newspapers, sexual advice columns, television programmes devoted to sexual relationship matters—television watching may also include scientific programmes on, say, hormone replacement therapy or prostate cancer).
- companionship/friendship—though this has not featured a great deal so far in our explorations it is obviously a major aspect which we will turn to in later parts of this book. It is frequently a goal positively portrayed in soaps and some films (e.g. the popular science fiction film *Cocoon* made it a key issue).
- pursuing exciting activities—could range from engaging in or watching local sporting competitions, to absailing and surfing, to taking substantial risks on the stock market, to watching a thrilling movie, in fact, anything which gets your adrenalin flowing.
- recreation—watching television, going to the movies, reading, listening to music, following sport as a spectator.
- optional—any *comfort* goal you think is important, but is not listed above.

2. Control

As before it is a matter of preference rather than exclusion, that is, what comes first, second, third, and so on. All the *control* goals may be important to you. Just try to rank them in order of importance.

- money—is meant to refer primarily to having or seeking a growing income, or expanding your wealth by some other means.
- status—refers to extent of public recognition, including being in the newspapers or on television, being secretary of the local sporting

club, standing for the council etc. It is about being called prime minister, doctor, professor, school principal, nurse, or teacher.
- control—is a more diffuse factor in your life and can range from your relationship with your children and partner, to your control over your working life; it is also about your independence and freedom of choice.
- power—is about control of others at home or at work.
- influence—can come from any of the above singularly or in combination; it is about getting other people to do what you want, even though you do not have the authority or means to directly control them, as you do with power.
- optional—any *control* goal you think is important, but is not listed above.

3. Creativity

Place in order of their importance to you the following:

- development—refers here to personal and professional development and growth; doing things to improve your personal and professional life (reading this book could contribute to both of these goals, as may watching an instructive television programme).
- enjoying aesthetic activities—refers in this checklist to being a willing observer at the theatre, opera, dance, ballet, musicals, films, galleries and museums (you might also have considered these in your comfort goals as recreation).
- creativity—refers to participating creatively in an activity which may include making a cake you had not made before, writing a poem, making a piece of furniture, designing a weaving pattern, making a skirt, building a bridge, painting a picture, and so on.
- productivity—refers to being satisfied with the paid or unpaid work in which you are engaged, seeing it as worthwhile, and enjoying it.
- optional—any *creativity* goal you think is important, but is not listed above.

Now you can make the broader choice of placing in order of importance, *comfort, control* and *creativity* themselves from one to three. This may be quite difficult, but just ponder long and hard. Which area do you spend most of your energy on? Which area currently brings you feelings of happiness and satisfaction?

You may want to include in your priority listing spiritual, religious or moral goals and associated activities. These could include any of the following: going to church, reading spiritual or uplifting books/magazines (these may not necessarily be religious), participating in some form of worship, praying or reflecting from a moral perspective on your life. If you wish to rank this you can compare it with your three main goals. Thus spiritual/moral goals would come somewhere from one to four in comparison with *comfort, control* and *creativity*.

Using the results of Exercise 2

The results you have obtained above will provide you with a picture of your happiness goals, in other words, what is most important to you at the moment. As you proceed through this book you may notice you want to change them—that's fine. They are your goals, your results, and clearly you can change them.

As with the previous exercise you will find it helpful to keep the results to use as a check against the ideas, suggestions and strategies provided in later chapters. You can then select from the approaches raised those which best suit your particular needs and those which match your goals.

You may find it helpful to compare your results with those of a trusted friend and consider how and why they differ. For example, if the other person chooses comfort as their main goal, it would be helpful to consider how they learnt this. What aspects of their experiences have influenced this choice— their parents, peers, media? Is their main goal different from yours? Can you say how you learnt yours? Are the goals that you have both chosen healthy ones? Will they contribute to or detract from your long-term wellbeing? Sometimes of course 'the devil is in the detail'. For example, you may want to look closely at the different emphases you have placed on particular aspects of comfort.

Hopefully you have now sorted out what goals you have at the moment and how you have learnt them. Doing this may have already caused you to change your goals and what you can do about attaining them. The remainder of this book is devoted to looking at how to reach your happiness destinations—either the goals you have identified in Exercise 2 or goals which evolve as you read on.

Being happy in a sustained way generally means more than getting what you want. Though you may be clear about what you want, you also need to be clear about the principles governing happiness that need to be taken into account when pursuing your goals. These principles are spelt out in the next chapter.

Summary

You have learnt that:

- the media has focused you and your teachers on a very wide range of messages—some that support your happiness goals and some that do not.
- half-truths and mixed messages can lead you astray.

And most importantly, you have established your own happiness goals.

PRINCIPLES OF HAPPINESS

While you may have a strong, even passionate, desire to fly a beautiful new kite, an attempt to fly it in a 70-km gale is likely to meet with disaster. The steps you take to achieve your goals need to be tempered with a good appreciation of the circumstances. For me to enter the high jump competition in the local athletics sports competition is not a good idea! No matter how much I would thrill to gliding over the bar, the realities of my physique demand I develop other desires. These examples may seem extreme but the point nonetheless is important. Often acceptance of life's circumstances is a key to living well.

Similarly what seems a course of action obviously in your best interests may not give you the result you expect. I know from experience and I bet you know too that what you set out to achieve, and sometimes do, may not provide the happiness you expected. This change from expectations to reality can be experienced in the big *and* little things of life; in relationships, a new job, and in the film that doesn't live up to its good reviews.

In the last chapter you worked out the kind of *comfort, control* and *creativity* targets you judged to be important. What you need to know is how to achieve such goals and whether you will feel happy when you reach them.

The eight principles of happiness which follow provide a framework to guide the achievement of your goals. Each principle is dealt with in more detail in Part 2 where strategies and approaches to apply the particular principle are suggested.

Principle 1: What you want may not be what you need

We've discussed how you may have learnt to seek experiences, which, in the end, serve your happiness goals poorly. At the simplest level you may have learnt to 'love' unhealthy foods, which, if consistently eaten, will be storing up not just fat but future unhappiness. This first principle encourages you not to rush into decisions, and to avoid certain impulse activities like buying fast food. It suggests that you may often need to pause and check to see if what you want is going to get you what you need. To check effectively you need to be aware of what you need—to know just how much food or sleep, for example, you require. You need also to know how to best manage the basic wants of life such as sex and comfort.

One key way of managing this principle is to ensure that there is balance in your life.

FOR EXAMPLE

There is a story from the Middle East that describes how two men about to be executed will win a reprieve if they can walk a tightrope across a deep canyon. The first man succeeds and the second calls to him asking how he did it. The first man calls back saying that all his life when things had been going too far to the right he moved back to the left and vice versa. For him, life had been a balancing act and he was practised in it.

Getting things in balance requires constant practice and is not something to do only in times of crisis. It can help to ensure that *wants* don't outstrip *needs*.

To get things in balance means to be conscious of the way you are distributing your time, attention, energy and enthusiasm. At one level this may mean pausing for ten minutes at the end of a week and reflecting on what you have done during the week and then specifically planning how you will distribute your time next week. In a longer-term way this can mean planning the key activities for the next month or year, ensuring that you allocate time to those pursuits you believe are important.

One way of achieving balance in your life is to counterbalance different aspects of your personality with your different, sometimes conflicting, wants. Martial arts' teachers talk about *being centred* with your two feet firmly on the ground ready to move in either direction. Living is a constant process of adjustment. If you find that your life is consumed by work, then you need to put more recreation into your life; if you notice that you are doing very little physical activity, then you need to spend a little time being active; if you find your thoughts are continually focused on one thing, then you need to use your mind to participate in other possibilities and so on.

A lack of time is one of the most common reasons we give for not engaging in self-help programmes or even activities we enjoy. Sometimes you may have to ask yourself what matters most. Generally, in making choices, one activity is given more importance than another: *I just cannot go on that morning walk, I have to get to work.* In some situations you would need to get up earlier, in others you may be able to rearrange your work times, or go for a walk in your lunch hour, after work, or in the evenings. What is possible depends on what you really want. (As someone who enjoys the comfort of that extra hour's unnecessary sleep I do know this quandary only too well!)

Another way to put this is to say that there are often times when a *need* should be placed before a *want*.

While the principle of *wants* and *needs* influences much of what you do and comes up in various parts of this book, it is especially

> A lack of time is one of the most common reasons we give for not engaging in self-help programmes or even activities we enjoy.

relevant to our basic desires. It is this aspect that is examined in Part 2, pages 59–79.

Principle 2: Trust your gut (notice your feelings and flashes of insight)

The more experience I have with people trying to improve the way they feel and develop new skills, the more I have come to feel that 'trust your initial gut feeling' is good advice. Sometimes the gut feeling is a twinge of fear or anger which may arrive after a suggestion that you are, say, incompetent in a particular task. To notice this is to recognise your own extra sensitivity—your self-doubt—and to be on track in the future to reduce its bad effect on the way you feel. Gut feelings urge you to notice the onset of fear and anger so that you can learn what they are 'telling' you.

If your gut feeling is fear or anger, don't automatically act to vent your feelings. For example, it is unwise to let your anger give rise to aggressive actions when you know 'in your gut' that the anger is misplaced.

This principle however does mean that you pay attention to your feelings, not only the emotional ones, but also those that tell you when you are tired, or upset, or when you have a flash of insight. To ignore such sources of learning may be to limit your capacity for positive change and future happiness.

Additionally Principle 2 looks at your intuitive feelings which can be based on knowledge that you may not even be aware that you have. To be aware of your feelings, your body talk and your intuition—to listen to it and respond to it— requires you to be body and feeling conscious. You need to be able to notice what you are feeling emotionally and physically without having these experiences overwhelm you. To do this you need to be emotionally fit.

'The more energy you spend the more you get' is a simple truth that most of us know. Anyone who trains for sport knows it, but perhaps you haven't often applied it to your daily living. In order to spend enormous amounts of energy, swimmers train for hours each day; athletes who are long-distance runners generally spend more time on the track than sprinters; and basketballers regularly sweat out their training in the stadium. You don't get less energy by going for that walk, but rather build yourself up to be able to be more energetic in the future.

Becoming emotionally strong is similar. You need to train your emotions on a regular basis to be emotionally stronger, and to be calm enough to listen attentively to the messages coming from your body. You need, for example, to participate in some form of relaxation training if you are going to be able to relax when you need to and to 'hear' what your feelings are telling you.

Principle 3: It is better to serve yourself than your ego

Sometimes your actions serve to enhance your ego. Many, what could be called 'false happiness goals', are based on ego. These can include actions taken and decisions made on the basis of a desire for, say, status, prestige, certain forms of control over others and many forms of personal indulgence. Of course, these gratifying experiences may be a byproduct of other activities—Einstein didn't set out to become famous, he set out to learn new ideas, to be creative. He became famous along the way. There are probably many actors who pursue their craft because this is what they enjoy doing. Some actors, now well known, spent ten to twenty years in obscurity before hitting the big-time.

From a very young age you began to separate yourself from other people and things in your environment. This idea of personal identity only becomes a problem when you develop ego-demands that are counter-productive to your more positive self-development. When, for example, you claim ownership of all the toys in the toy box! Nevertheless, unless you are quite remarkable, it is inevitable that you develop some ego-goals along the way.

One way of minimising the potential negative effect of ego-goals on your happiness is to improve your self-appreciation. The setbacks that happen in everyone's life can be better managed, if you value yourself. Similarly, a person with high self-esteem is less likely to be motivated by a desire for status or prestige. The person who boasts the most about their abilities, who shouts the loudest at card parties, or who most frequently claims credit for work success, may be the one with the greatest ego problems and the least self-appreciation.

Thus strong self-esteem gives you confidence and the ability to take knocks and diminish ego-goals and demands, leading you to more personal *control* over what you do and to greater happiness. Ways to improve your self-esteem are dotted throughout this book as well as the section specifically on this topic (pages 06–9). Perhaps one of the key ways to boost self-esteem is to recognise your own growth and achievements.

Exercise 3: Recognising small successes

- Keep a small notebook that can be fitted into a pocket or handbag.
- Jot down your achievements on a daily basis. They can be anything, from simple successes with household jobs, to getting a date with someone you like, to collecting vegetables from your garden, to a comment of praise from the boss, to asking a question in a discussion (when you ordinarily wouldn't), or more comprehensive successes such as making a go-cart for your child, completing an adult education course, or planning a new room on your house.

Principle 4: Happiness is growth

Happiness is not remaining stationary. That way lies stagnation. In seeking and meeting new challenges, you can grow and become more confident, satisfied and controlled. Dealing effectively with either good or bad life experiences gives you opportunities for growth.

Learning is part of that growth. One of the keys to successful personal development is through continued learning, whether it is new *skills* (e.g. by teaching yourself or being taught computer applications, or by discovering better ways to grow roses, or by learning how to train and handle dogs), or new *ideas* (e.g. keeping up with events in the news, listening to information on radio and television, reading).

Improving your knowledge and skills will make your self-esteem grow! To grow personally, successive steps are usually necessary. Sometimes you can be put off because a desirable goal seems so far away or, on the other hand, you may try to do too many things in a short period of time.

There are two sides to this. The first is that you cannot go down, say, six paths at the same time. When choosing to change some part of your life it is probably best to focus on one aspect, rather than trying to improve several different ones. Thus it is enough to work on improving feeling more relaxed and calm, rather than *also* trying to improve your assertiveness, practise self-approving affirmations and follow a plan to give up smoking. Even within a particular path such as relaxation, it is usually also best to practise the one approach, say, stomach breathing, as opposed to trying other relaxation techniques at the same time.

The second point is that it is sensible to take one step at a time down the path you have chosen rather than pushing too hard to reach the end of the road. Like that old joke: 'How do you eat an elephant?' The answer is: 'One bite at a time.' Patience and persever-

Improving your knowledge and skills will make your self-esteem grow!

ance are required from each of us. To achieve sustained change often means sustained practice. You may not sometimes notice the changes you are making in the short term so you need to be wary of not being discouraged.

Principle 5: Others matter

We all know we cannot easily live our lives in isolation from others. It is only a few rare beings who choose to live solitary lives. Even in strict religious orders, separated from the rest of the group, monks and nuns live in communities. We are social creatures.

There is general agreement among psychologists that your personal happiness is bound up with the happiness of others. The more you accept this, the less you are able to support the impulsive, individual ego-focused messages used by some forms of media and advertising.

Even if you behave purely from a self-centred view you need to take account of the concerns and happiness of others as their wellbeing affects you. It is now suggested in scientific circles that you actually become mentally in-tune, through resonating brainwaves, with people who you closely associate with—you become literally 'on the same wavelength' and thus affected by them. Just living life for yourself may not produce the result you expect.

In pursuit of happiness goals, you need to be able to relate effectively to others. Go to Principle 5 (pages 141–162) to find more detailed ways of recognising and responding to the principle that others matter.

Principle 6: Knowing is rarely enough

Most of us, when presented with a useable idea can say, 'Yes. I understand that. I can see that's the way to go.' Actually changing what you do is often a more difficult task. If you want to be happier, *you need to do something different*. If your past way of doing things had worked, you would be satisfied with the way things are.

This principle is especially relevant to the entrenched behaviours that you may wish to change. As a former smoker, I made a number of attempts to change the habit before eventually being successful. It is also true for firmly established ways of reacting, such as continually using the same unsuccessful techniques to get your resident teenager to turn down the music—shouting at them can give you some temporary personal relief and may even result in a temporary decrease in the CD player's volume, but it doesn't often result in a sustained decrease in noise output. You probably know that shouting doesn't work, but to change this you need to know not only other ways of behaving, but also to have the capacity, the desire, and the energy to apply them. This can be learnt.

Principle 7: Learn how to change your mind (and how you feel)

FOR EXAMPLE

A scientific observer of groups once reported on a cult that predicted the end of the world on a certain date. Members of the cult waited on a mountain for the end to come. The observer predicted that the cult would collapse when the designated time had passed and nothing had happened. He was wrong. The belief of members of the cult actually became stronger as they worked out reasons why the end hadn't happened.

Sometimes changing your mind is a very difficult thing to do. You may continue to find reasons why your initial ideas were right even in the face of disproving evidence. Nonetheless if you are to reach your happiness goals you may have to re-evaluate some of your ideas—you may need sometimes to change your mind.

You may be able to refocus by paying attention to some other aspect of your life, while not rejecting the old belief immediately. This can also come from trusting your creative side when your actions don't *feel* right. Sometimes it can come from recognising, in a more reasoned way, when the evidence becomes too great to reject, that your old thoughts are not matching (not congruent with) your new thoughts.

FOR EXAMPLE

When, for example, your *old thought* is, say, that 'saving is unimportant', but that you find as the consequence of your spendthrift behaviour that you are continually unable to have the things that your friends are getting. A *new thought* may be that it would be a good idea to have a fair bit more outdoor recreation and therefore to have some camping equipment. However, this is in conflict with the actions that come from your *old thought*. The next *new thought* could be that 'saving may be required'. Notice this is a measured movement not completely rejecting the old thought. You are not, for example, saying that 'saving is essential', only that that there could be situations where it may be needed.

Sometimes changing how you *feel* will also assist you to change what you do. It may even affect how you think. To become more comfortable with flying (when you have been decidedly uncomfortable) may affect not only your interest in distant holidays, but your willingness to participate in a business which involves air travel, and therefore your attitude towards your career also changes.

Even one small change in what you do can be the start of something big. In fact, there is a view recently expressed by some biologists that at a certain point in time, in the development of a species, when circumstances have been built up in readiness, a small change can result in a dramatic development. It is a bit like when the removal of one small piece of snow creates an avalanche. *With you, too, everything counts*; first, as you build up for change, and second, when the last little piece tips you into a big shift in your life. What you do, however small, matters. You can change in order to achieve your happiness goals little by little, or in big chunks.

Principle 8: Use the ideas of great teachers

For thousands of years, spiritual teachers have developed their philosophies on happiness. They have said that by behaving in certain ways you will attain happiness, if not in this life, then in a next. Their beliefs, you are told, will lead you to a more comfortable, congruent, content, or harmonious existence—not one necessarily free of pain, but one in which the pain is bearable. You are expected to be able to achieve this through exercising control over your life, whether through an effort of will on your part, or through the grace of God (or some other benevolent being), or through the practices that they advocate.

Putting aside for a moment individual theologies, many spiritual teachings and views on love, on finding meaning in your life, on understanding others and on living effectively, have much to offer and can in many ways be seen to be consistent with certain aspects of contemporary understanding. It makes sense to look at their views to see what can be learnt to help you in the pursuit of happiness, regardless of your religious stance.

Especially important in most teachings is the concept of *not surrendering your personal control* to other people who have dishonourable intentions, that is, people seeking your support, physically, financially or emotionally for activities against others—in old-fashioned religious language 'the purveyors of evil'. Obvious examples include: allowing, or even supporting, a bully to beat up another person, partially bankrolling a project which you know would leave people homeless, standing by and not saying anything when one person gives another an emotionally damaging tongue lashing. More subtle examples could include: surrendering control to another by supporting their addiction, as distinct from supporting them; allowing yourself to be persuaded by someone close to you to, say, lie to others, or to keep the purse you found with 60 pounds in it.

Your sense of personal happiness can benefit from certain religious ideas and practices. The observance of moral strictures like those discussed above often helps you feel internally consistent and ensures that your behaviour is in tune with your values—not always easy but when achieved it is guaranteed to make you feel good!

Even creativity, one of our happiness goals, can be seen to be indirectly promoted by religion, *when and if* the particular religious practices, such as prayer or meditation, lead to a more relaxed, less tense way of living. Additionally, 'listening' to internal spiritual messages can in one sense be viewed as a source of creative behaviour.

Further reading on Principle 8 (pages 200–23) expands on these issues and provides some practices that are very helpful.

The Dragon Principle

The emperors of ancient China had a special number—nine. This number also had great significance in wider society. And they had the dragon as a symbol of power. I have called the last and ninth principle of happiness the Dragon Principle because it is powerful and is related to all the other principles.

The Dragon Principle is: *all principles are interrelated*.

Each principle can be related in different ways to each other principle. You can, for example, break the third principle by serving your ego-goals above the needs of yourself or your partner and so at the same time be breaking the fifth principle that others matter. Perhaps you apply for a promotion (control goal) in the south of the country where you know that you will have to spend several hours commuting every day and that your work performance will be lowered (not serving yourself), and that your partner has long-term commitments in the north.

A more positive interconnection of princi-ples exists when you identify and place your needs above your wants and make time to undertake a learning activity that promotes your growth. You could, for example, restruc-ture your work time, leaving half an hour early on Wednesdays so that you can attend that 5.00 p.m. course, foregoing your after-work coffee and cake. Thus placing your needs above your wants (Principle 1) and promoting growth through learning (Principle 4).

The Dragon Principle is: *all principles are interrelated.*

PART 2

PRINCIPLE 1
WHAT YOU WANT MAY NOT BE
WHAT YOU NEED

The Dragon Principle tells you that the tension between what you want and what you need to build long-term happiness is applicable to most parts of your life. In this chapter it is the *basic* wants and needs of your body that are the main focus. These are the ones most associated with your physical *comfort* goals.

Our desire for food, sex, sleep, and to feel well, is natural. However, these needs become influenced by what you have learnt you should want. While individual needs will vary, the media in its many forms tries to guess what they might be as well as sending messages which seek to influence you. Their views become a common denominator, providing you with a ready-made range of expectations on how basic needs should be satisfied. In the discussion which follows the media has therefore been used as one way of identifying expectations and wants, especially those that may not be what you need.

What you put in your mouth

Food, drink (and cigarettes)
There are plenty of mixed messages about food and drink:

- Being beautiful is advertised as almost synonymous with being happy. Being beautiful means being a certain shape and size and this means eating certain food and doing certain kinds of exercise. Yet we see beautiful people eating low-fat yoghurt, and beautiful people eating chips and chocolate biscuits. And of course, being beautiful is not in itself a recipe for happiness—what people think is beautiful is often a matter of fashion, history or culture. Today, unnaturally coloured hair and body piercing seems the rage with lots of people under thirty!

- Cooking can be great fun! Delighting your taste buds is always enjoyable. It is a regular feature of living, as is the need to control your weight. In most newsagents and bookshops, cooking books occupy a substantial portion of the shelf space, and dietary books generally take a major part of the health section. Clearly eating a balanced diet will help you to feel healthy and therefore feel good. However, what do I do with all my old cookbooks? Should I have my diet first or my meal?!

- Drinking (alcohol) is great for your social life you are told—it can take you out of yourself. You are asked to believe that it is at least as good as going to a tropical island; that you can have as much fun as polar bears at a party; that it is a definite sexual turn-on—none of which are probably true. The currently expressed medical view is that drinking in moderation four or five times a week may be okay for men; less for women.

- In the bad old days, there was a message that said that enjoying the great outdoors went with enjoying a cigarette. These days tobacco companies are having a much harder time of it. There are people who are now suing the companies because of their present state of ill-health. Those original messages can now be seen as promoting behaviour which is likely to be detrimental to your health.

There is a particularly persuasive view that suggests you satisfy your basic physical desires by attending to them immediately. It is well represented in a form of advertising that borrows some of its language from public demonstrations and protests: 'What do we want? When do we want it?—Now!' It is a view which advocates immediate control of a situation. It can relate to food, drink, and often by implication, to sex.

This approach suggests that happiness is achieved through quick direct action, it ignores that in many instances the consequences of such actions can produce substantial unhappiness in the longer term. It also often ignores by implication the feelings of others whose happiness is tied up with yours.

Like other mixed messages, the idea is half true. Living spontaneously *when* there are no personal consequences or problems for other people is fine. Don't worry, be aware of the moment, and enjoy it. The issue is when do you apply this approach? Because you don't apply it all the time. Responding to your enjoyment of alcohol by getting drunk frequently, for example, is not a recipe for long-term or even short-term happiness. This issue is explored in more detail in Principle 6 (pages 163–82).

FOR EXAMPLE
I once had a friend who said that if wasn't for hangovers he would have been a drunk.

To achieve a happy balance in eating and drinking it is necessary to recognise what you need, without your view of this being fogged by *wants* that you have learnt from all your teachers. You can get this clarity by first checking out what distortions of your basic needs you have learnt. This can be done by noticing how you think about food, by recognising you are being told something about food or drink in what you see, hear or read and asking yourself if you agree with it. You can also actively seek out information that corrects ideas which seek to influence you but which you are aware are probably wrong. Ex-smokers are generally people who have eventually accepted ideas about the dangers of smoking as opposed to its joys. Similarly ideas of a balanced food and drink intake are a necessary step before taking action to change your lifestyle to implement these ideas. When the opportunity arises read, watch or listen to what you know are sensible views. Ones which assist you to hear the positive messages for your long-term happiness.

A second key aspect is listening to your body. This topic is discussed in more detail and in a different way in Principle 2. While you probably have the capacity to listen to your body talk, you may have learnt to ignore it, often to the detriment of your happiness.

You can see children who recognise when they have had enough to eat and those who seem deaf to the message that their body is giving them about being full. As an adult, you can probably recognise when you have had enough, although you may need some retraining if for years you haven't been listening.

Animals in their natural state rarely over-eat. It is only when we adopt them as pets and control their eating that they can be overfed.

Sometimes you may not even recognise when you need a drink (the non-alcoholic kind I mean!). In the summer heat you may get thirsty and look for a drink, but there are other times when you may not recognise the signals your body gives you telling you that you need fluid. Then you can become a little dehydrated and get a headache.

Julie's story: Paying attention to food

Julie had grown up in a family where eating wasn't a problem—everyone did it well! She was a friendly person who, in days gone by, would have been described as 'pleasantly plump'. However, at this stage of her life, after several failed dieting attempts, she was keen to lose weight. Instead of going to see a dietician she came to see me, mostly because I had been recommended by a client who was a friend of hers, but also perhaps because she knew that losing weight was something that involved more than counting calories.

Her weight had caused her to voluntarily restrict some of her life activities—she didn't go out much and was reluctant to attend a course she was thinking of doing. Despite this she wasn't someone who yearned to wear the latest fashion.

At her first visit we talked about the facts of eating, including how we rarely listen to our body needs, how we learn our eating habits, and the problems involved with dieting. We discussed some of the issues of relating to others with respect to food.

For the next week, her task was to pay attention to what she was eating, when she was eating, and to try to eat more slowly. When Julie rang me to change her next appointment time, she discussed how much more relaxed she felt because she didn't have a calorie target to reach but that even so she had started to change the food she was eating.

In a few more sessions she learnt some relaxation skills and that long-term change was a lifestyle matter including eating patterns.

The key for Julie was the effect that paying attention had on her poor eating habits (she always knew what was the best food for her) and the recognition that the weight loss could then take place over time.

I heard from Julie again about six months later; she had lost a few kilos, enrolled in a naturopathy course and, perhaps most importantly, she was feeling good about her life and herself.

Exercise 4: Noticing some basic needs

- In the next three days, bring into play your basic needs by trying to recognise, during eating, when you feel that you are no longer hungry.

- It helps to eat slowly.
- Try to smell your food first and chew it slowly noticing the flavours and the textures.
- You might also try to notice if you are hungry before you start eating.
- Similarly, say, three times each day, you could pause and check if your body is telling you that you need a drink.

Sex

What you want and expect of yourself sexually is coloured by what you are told is possible and, according to some sources, what you have a 'responsibility' to offer.

One view on sex commonly broadcast, particularly in magazines, is that you should be having sex frequently, with consummate skill and variation, and with someone who is desirable and attractive. While you might consider you have an attractive partner, you may find it difficult to match all the sexual exploits described in the media. Jumping off the wardrobe onto the bed, or such like, is not a usual activity in many households! The expectations generated for both men and women often involve considerable performance and frequent participation.

Another view promulgated since the sixties is one of sexual independence, freedom and having sex for the pleasure it gives you as an individual. A view that was sometimes presented in the past by stars like Madonna and any number of male pop-stars. Also it is an idea which can be seen as a reaction to the history of control of one partner by the other, particularly of women by men. Our concern here is whether such an approach brings happiness. The weight of anecdotal evidence about people who have many uncommitted sexual liaisons is that in the long run this lifestyle doesn't tend to produce the general well-being you are likely to be seeking. It is more than likely to lead to an increase in cravings, dissatisfaction with the results of sexual exploits and a failure to achieve other happiness goals.

Sexual behaviour is an important factor in most relationships and some reasonable level of competency is necessary. However, sex seems to work best in a context where there are a range of other factors supporting the couple's feelings and interactions with each other, rather than as a solely self-focused exercise.[1] Thus good sex can come from a relationship where love is expressed in a range of other forms of support, encouragement and partnership.

We have inherited a set of circumstances where:

- Sexual activity is not restricted in terms of timing—historically this was because it was not known when ovulation occurred, but now there are many forms of contraception.
- Paternity is best guaranteed by faithfulness—until only recently a woman with several partners could not always be sure who was the father of her child. Similarly, a man who had several partners could not be sure that any children born were his, unless he was sure that the sexual activity of his female partners was limited to him (a harem was one way of doing that!). Even with modern contraception methods, uncertainties continue to be settled in the courts; blood tests and DNA tests have been used to determine disputes about paternity.

Because sexual arousal can occur at any time whenever the appropriate sensory triggers are present (sight, sound, touch or smell), it can pose a threat to faithfulness. This dilemma has been the source of inspiration for many a novel and a significant contributor to much unhappiness—dis*comfort* and loss of *control*. There are frequent stories of politicians, and others, whose sexual urges have caused upheaval in their lives.

The problem for you is that such urges may occur at inconvenient times when you least want them, or you may decide to enjoy their fruits in circumstances which you later come to regret.

You can seek out these triggers, you can come across them incidentally or because someone shows them to you, or you can avoid or ignore them. Part of your task is being conscious of what is happening before you become fully engaged. Even something that springs from a purely biological impulse may not be what you need at that particular time. The exercise which follows is to help you sort out the extent and nature of the presence of these desires in your life. This is a first step in deciding which ones you actually need.

Exercise 5: Living with your sexual triggers

- To do this exercise you will need a small notebook that you can fit into your pocket or handbag.
- On each page have four columns representing the four categories of sexual triggers listed below.
- Over the next three days keep a record by placing a tick in the appropriate column when:

  1. You have sensory sexual triggers put in front of you (e.g. in advertising, in the news).
  2. You seek out triggers (e.g. watching particular people, turning to a particular part of the newspaper, watching certain television programmes, selecting certain videos).
  3. Triggers occur incidentally (e.g. by catching a glimpse of a particular man or woman, noticing the touch of a particular person, or you may have a memory that is triggered by association).
  4. You have avoided or ignored a trigger (e.g. by not turning on a particular programme when it was known to be on, or not buying a particular magazine when you knew it was available, or by 'turning off' the trigger and 'switching on' to something else).

- From your *comfort* and *control* points of view alone, leaving aside any moral issues, note which of the triggers resulted in an actual sexual response, and which did not.

- Which of the triggers supported your current happiness goals, and which were distractions? Which, by the nature and timing of their occurrence, were uncomfortable?
- Did you find that you had any control of your feelings? Could you switch to something else if you wanted to, as in point 4 above?

Clearly living a satisfying sexual life is, I suspect, one of your happiness goals. It is the rare person who can be celibate and content. Even Gandhi who was reputedly celibate for much of his married life is said to have complained of what teenagers used to call 'wet dreams'.

Placing your sexual needs before your sexual wants can probably be reduced to two points:

- Don't be seduced by public messages into believing you have some golden standard of performance to achieve in appearance, participation and technique, which measures you as a lesser human being if you don't achieve it—that way lies lower self-esteem and even poorer performance. This is not to say that you cannot learn to do some things differently—just don't make too much of that media hype.
- Understand that an enduring satisfying sexual life seems to occur most often within the context of an enduring effective relationship. For more on relationships, go to Principle 5, page 141.

Sleep

To want to have a good night's sleep is a common wish; to complain that you didn't get a good night's sleep is a common complaint. If your sleep expectations do not match your reality you are in good company. Around five to ten per cent of the population report that they experience sleeping difficulties on a regular basis; you too have probably had times when you had difficulty sleeping.

What you need and how to get more of what you need are explored next by looking at the facts and suggesting ways to improve sleep quality.

The amount of time needed in bed asleep varies from person to person. The normal range of time sleeping is approximately six to nine hours. Each of us tends to have an amount of time which satisfies us—thus you may regularly sleep eight hours a night, if you get less you feel tired. The quality of sleep is important. To have seven hours of good quality sleep is as good or better than nine hours of poor quality sleep. The test of the success of your sleep is measured generally in the extent of your day-time energy or tiredness. Being asleep is not simply the time you spend in bed, but rather the time you spend in bed actually asleep.

For your improved comfort it is worth noting these facts:

- Sleep is cyclic—most people wake several times a night (however briefly) even if they do not remember it; and sleep is not solid, it is not continuous.
- Most people dream, even if they do not remember it.
- Waking up during the night can potentially be disturbing. Your body may be aroused during dreaming, rapid eye movement (REM) sleep, which often occurs just before waking. When you are physically alert in the middle of the night it can make what you are thinking about seem more worrisome than it would ordinarily be. It is often worth remembering that things will seem better in the morning.
- You may misjudge the amount of sleep you are getting.
- Sleep is a particularly strong need; if you don't get enough on any one or two occasions you will usually catch up in the next day or so—not necessarily by getting an extra amount of sleep exactly replacing what you lost, but often by getting an improved quality of sleep with *some* extra sleeping time.

If you have difficulty going to sleep or you wake up excessively early, this can sometimes be attributed to your body rhythms. In your natural state, you would ordinarily have been exposed to plenty of morning light. If you do not have this, your internal clock may adjust so that sleep does not seem to be needed until the early hours of the morning. Similarly, if you walk around in the evening in semi-darkness, with, say, just the television on, your body clock may treat this period as if you have been asleep, and so when you go to bed you wake up after only a few hours. To manage this problem some scientists have introduced light therapy, which is based on exposing the person to excessive light in the form of a bank of fluoro-lights either in the morning or the evening, depending on whether the sleeping problem is going to sleep or waking early.

TIPS
To improve sleeping, you need to:

Remember
- Remember the facts.
- Remember that you can lose some sleep and catch up without special treatment.
- Remember that the true test of whether you are getting enough sleep is your level of day-time alertness. If you are not frequently sleepy and can perform your daily chores and work to a good standard, then you are probably getting enough sleep.
- Remember in the suggestions given below that what works for one person will not always work for another—find what suits you.

Do
- Avoid stimulating drinks (e.g. coffee) after your evening meal and limit your overall intake of caffeine to, say, five cups of tea or coffee during the day.
- Limit your smoking, if you are a smoker— nicotine, like caffeine,

is a stimulant.

- Allow yourself time to wind down before going to bed. Don't go to bed just after you have watched a horror movie or done your taxes—walk more slowly around the house—listen to soothing music.
- Use the bedroom only for sleeping and sexual activity. Don't watch TV or read in bed for long periods on a regular basis.
- If you should wake during the night do not stay in bed awake for more than ten minutes—get up, make yourself a warm drink, read something boring or non-stimulating (parts of the daily newspaper can be good for this!). Go back to bed only when you are starting to feel sleepy; walk slowly back to bed.
- Get up at the same time each day, if you can, irrespective of what time you go to bed; if you are tired you can go to bed earlier that night.
- Make sure that you get plenty of bright morning light when you get up each morning and that at night you do not have several hours of semi-darkness in your house before going to bed.
- Try physical activity; if during the day you have been for a long walk, a swim, or played a game of tennis, your chances of getting a good night's sleep will be greatly increased.
- Learn and practise some relaxation techniques described in the next chapter.
- The reason why counting sheep has been a favourite suggestion is that it is a boring relaxant, although I am not sure these days how many people find it works for them. Try an imagination method:

    1. Imagine there is a blackboard in front of you: you can see on the right-hand side a circle with a 100 in it and on the left the word 'sleep' is written in block capitals; in your mind, first trace slowly over the word 'sleep', then with an imaginary duster rub out the number 100 without touching the edge of the circle and replace it with the number 99; keep repeating this sequence.
    2. When you are in bed go backwards through the day in

> your mind (i.e. start with the last thing that happened
> before you went to bed, and then go to the second last
> thing, and so on, gradually going back through the day to
> morning). In other words, you literally 'unwind' your day.

Of course, there are particular sleep problems that will require medical attention. In most countries, there are also sleep laboratories that offer special help.

Feeling well

Wanting to feel well is a normal and expected happiness target. This is a positive goal as well as a desire to be free from pain. Your expectations about your health and how to meet them, like your need for food, sex and sleep, are likely to have been coloured by what you have learnt. Again, you need to be cautious, checking that what you have learnt to want is really what you need.

It is almost self-evident that you need some exercise and a sensible balanced diet to feel well.

A little of what you fancy . . .
Perhaps a major stressor in our lives is trying hard to follow every suggestion anyone makes to improve our health and wellbeing! Associates for Research Into the Science of Enjoyment (ARISE) confirm what many of us already know—that if you attempt to follow too many rigid restrictive health rules you can make your life miserable.[2] It is always best to enjoy some of life's small pleasures and avoid becoming a healthaholic. Sensible doses of pleasure lower stress and strengthen the immune system.

Walking, running, jumping and standing still
Our bodies have evolved to suit periods of activity and periods of inactivity. It is only in the last one hundred years that large numbers of us have experienced highly sedentary ways

of living. As well as being good for your heart (for most people), *enjoyable* exercise reduces your stress levels and increases your capacity to relax.

Food and diet

The messages associated with food and diet are also health issues. There is a strong medical view that the cycle of dieting, putting weight back on, and dieting again can be bad for your long-term health. It is known that if you lose weight, you lose some muscle and that generally when you put weight back on you put on fat. If you do this in a cyclic way you increase your quantity of fat and decrease your muscle. This does not help you with your long-term comfort.

Pain

An aspect of feeling well is your experience of pain. It is likely that you will experience occasional bouts of pain during your life. It is also probable that you will have had smaller aches and pains that you sometimes noticed and at other times ignored. Fortunately, you will have probably had long periods relatively pain-free.

Pain is a tool of the body preventing further damage and signalling a need to take suitable remedial action.

While different expert views exist, pain continues to be seen by some as a necessary part of our lives. At the simplest level, the fact that you can recognise the sensation of heat and the production of pain at a certain point prevents you from, say, more seriously burning yourself on a stove. Even people with chronic pain caused by physical injury will sometimes say that the pain prevents them from twisting and turning in a different way and causing more damage to their body. Viewed in this way, pain is a tool of the body preventing further damage and signalling a need to take suitable remedial action.

TIPS

- Techniques suggested to assist relaxation and to relieve tension and stress in Principle 2 can also be used to diminish pain experiences. Indeed some pain can be experienced because of the stresses you may have placed on your muscles or jaws or brain (as in tension headaches).

- It is often your perception of pain that tells you what to feel. The way you notice pain influences how keenly you feel it. It is not surprising, therefore, that the approaches sometimes used are ones that distract you from the pain, or offer alternative ways of 'seeing' or 'feeling' it. People with frequent pain will sometimes, if they can manage it, use concentration on a task, such as a craft activity or solving a problem on a computer, to distract them from attending to the pain messages. A therapist may suggest to you that a pain you feel is 'sharp like a knife' could feel like the pressure of someone poking you with a blunt instrument. Such a suggestion does not remove the pain, but could change the way you feel it.

- Another aspect of your perception is how you seek to deal with it mentally. If you say to yourself, 'This is awful, it must go away, I cannot cope,' then the feeling of the pain may seem more severe than if you give yourself more positive messages like, 'It will pass. I'll manage. I'll get on with something else.' While it may be difficult at times to use the more positive sayings, sometimes called *coping self-talk*, the negative sayings are worse in that they can intensify the pain feelings you are experiencing.

Apart from what you can do yourself, there are medical, psychological and allied health approaches that will minimise the experience of pain. You may need to explore these other avenues until you find something that works for you.

Sometimes what you want and sometimes what you need—a media experience

The various forms of the media can vicariously provide

aspects of what you want or need. Whether they are helpful to you depends on how you use them.

One particular feature of the media over the last forty years has been television and the increasing amount of time that people spend watching it. Many studies have shown that school-aged children will spend more time watching television than going to school.

As adults most of us generally spend several hours a day watching television. In terms of time, television is the media of choice. If you are watching voluntarily then it is reasonable to think that this is a source of entertainment and pleasure that comes high on your happiness *comfort* scale. It can also be seen as a source of hand-held power and control (I sometimes wonder about that channel-switching, predominantly male, behaviour). It can also be seen as an escape from pain (psychological and even physical) and is in this sense another source of comfort.

Sometimes the potential of television to act as an escape can mean that it is used to excess, like an addiction, soothing wounds and distracting you from actions that may lead to more enduring happiness. While ultimately it is only you that can determine whether the happiness television provides is something you need rather than merely want, it is worth seeing how it can be used to serve your *wants* as well as your *needs*.

Television can be an escape from psychological and even physical pain.

As I suspect you know, television is easy—all you need to do is switch it on. The television is part of our security, a constant factor in our lives and family households. Its stories reassure. Like *Punch and Judy* and the miracle and morality plays of hundreds of years ago, the television soaps tell stories in everyday language, and perhaps impart their version of the path to present-day salvation and happiness.

So the television is capable of being a substantial source of *comfort* (and a small source of *control*), but it also offers something to the viewer by way of creativity, development and productivity in its informative, aesthetic and how-to-do-it programmes. It is interesting that it is the rare person who admits to being an avid watcher. How many people do you know who will tell you they love television? Who has said to you recently, 'I am so glad my children spend hours each day in front of our television'?[3]

You may be suspicious of what television offers and feel guilty because you believe others may think that you are turning into a couch potato; or that you are leaving your child-rearing responsibilities to the 'third parent'; or that you are not exercising your mind; or that you are being lazy and distracted from the jobs you should be doing.

Even though at times you may get further down the track towards your happiness goals by turning off the set, it is still important not to feel guilty about watching. Feeling guilty can trap you into sadness and it rarely achieves anything. One way of avoiding feeling guilty is to recognise that many others are in the same boat as you.

Of course, watching television so much that you have little time to spare for other goals is unlikely to be satisfying. One way of recognising the predominance of television in your life is to consider the importance you attach to it and other forms of recreation. The following exercise explores your recreational goals.

Exercise 6: Time on media happiness

This exercise is probably best shared with others. You could invite a few friends to do it. You don't all need to do it at the one time but you can compare notes afterwards. If you do it as a family, you are asked to let each person have his or her own version of the truth—do not tell your teenage son he has got his facts wrong and that he actually watches television twelve hours a day, not two! This is meant to be an exercise in your pursuit of happiness, not a recipe for a family brawl. Similarly, comparing answers between family members or friends at the end of the exercise is an opportunity to discover more about your goals rather than judge the goals of others.

Step 1

Circle a number against each of the following media activities. The numbers, high to low, are to show how important you think each activity is. How valuable a contribution does it make to your happiness (both short- and long-term)? Thus 1 is highly valued, 2 is fairly highly valued, 3 is valued, 4 is indifferent, 5 is slightly rejected, 6 is strongly rejected, 7 is completely rejected.

Reading a book for recreation 1 2 3 4 5 6 7

Reading a magazine 1 2 3 4 5 6 7

Going to a cinema 1 2 3 4 5 6 7

Watching videos 1 2 3 4 5 6 7

Going to the theatre (plays/musicals/ballet/opera) 1 2 3 4 5 6 7

Watching television—recreational 1 2 3 4 5 6 7

Watching television—instructional 1 2 3 4 5 6 7

Listening to music (radio, CDs or tapes) 1 2 3 4 5 6 7

Listening to radio— recreational 1 2 3 4 5 6 7

Listening to radio—instructional 1 2 3 4 5 6 7

Following sport on television or radio 1 2 3 4 5 6 7

Going to a sporting event as a spectator 1 2 3 4 5 6 7

Note: the activities may overlap—instructional television may also be recreational; just mark them in order of importance to you, numbering them according to your initial response.

Step 2

Name the first three television programmes you can think of:

_____

_____

_____

Name the last film you saw:

_____

Name whether the last piece of music you listened to was happy, sad, funny, or other:

_____

Name the last sporting event you listened to or watched:

_____

Step 3

Write down the amount of time (your best guess) you spent during the last fortnight on:

Reading a book _____

Reading a magazine _____

Reading a newspaper _____

Listening to the radio _____

Watching television _____

Watching videos _____

Listening to music _____

Going out to the cinema or theatre, including plays, musicals, ballet, or opera _____

Going to a sporting event as a spectator _____

Using the results

You can use your results in a number of ways. You can, for example, simply examine your answers to see what they may tell you about the importance you place on particular forms of media. You can compare your answers in Step 1 and Step 3. Are you spending your time on those activities (Step 3) which you say in Step 1 are most important to your happiness? You can compare notes with family and friends. This is a fun activity! Laughter, as I am sure you have noticed, is very much part of happiness. You should also be able to note that while there are probably differences between your answers and those of your friends or family, there are also probably common threads (e.g. on which activities did most of you spend the most time? On which activities did most of you spend the least time?). Finally you can check if what you are doing is what you need. If you never read a book although it is high on your list in Step 1, just do it! Go to the bookshelf/ library/bookshop right *now*!

You should keep your results so that you can in the future, if you wish to, change your time arrangements for your media activities. Perhaps they can be better arranged to meet your own happiness goals?

A particular issue for some parents is how much television their children watch. TV-watching is likely to be strongly influenced by the presence (or lack) of desirable alternatives. For children, this often means activities that others, including parents, are doing. The more your child can participate in your activities and is encouraged to do so with praise and patient help, the less time they will have for television. Additionally, having family rules that are consistently followed by all members can generate good TV-watching habits. The key is consistency by everyone.

Paying attention

The key to managing your wants is to take it easy and pay attention. If you eat your food slowly noticing what you are doing, not only are you likely to take in amounts closer to what you need, but you are also more likely to actually get more pleasure out of eating. To eat a hamburger on the run, or to gobble it down while reading the newspaper or driving a car is to diminish your opportunity to enjoy it. Of course as you pay more attention to your eating you may change your eating patterns to make them more consistent with what you actually need.

Similarly drinking, sex and exercise may be enjoyed more, if you do them more leisurely, rather than according to some prepackaged 'fast food' practice.

In your television viewing you also need to be conscious of what is happening and whether the programme you're watching is leading you to meet your basic *needs* or just temporarily satisfying unproductive *wants*.

Summary

You have learnt that:

- you may have developed 'wants' for, say, certain kinds of food or sex and that these learnt cravings can distort your recognition of your basic needs.
- there are ways of noticing your needs better and that by recognising what is happening in your life (say, with your sexual triggers) you can find the means to respond more comfortably.
- sleep is a need you can manage.
- pain too can be managed in ways that are more helpful rather than ones that make the pain more debilitating.
- how you use the media, especially television, needs to be assessed to see how it is contributing to what you need, rather than just to what you want.

PRINCIPLE 2
TRUST YOUR GUT (NOTICE YOUR FEELINGS AND FLASHES OF INSIGHT)

Paying attention to your physical needs, as described in Principle 1, is part of listening to your body talk. Often your emotional feelings, too, will come to you as an experience in your body such as butterflies in the stomach, a tension headache, getting hot and bothered, feeling high, or feeling numb or weak. These sensations are often subtle indications of fear or anger.

In a different way, you may feel you know intuitively that this person is not right for that job, or that you can respond well to that person, or that you should not go on that holiday.

This chapter explores how you can recognise and use your emotional feelings and gain more access to your intuitive wisdom. It is a common sense rule that improving your self-knowledge will improve your chances of happiness.

Fright, flight and fight

Understanding the nature of two common feelings, fear and anger, will help to show you what your choices are when you 'hear' them. For our human ancestors' survival it was important to be able to respond rapidly, perhaps without thinking.

When they came out of a cave or down from a tree to be suddenly confronted by a bear or a tiger, a number of automatic body responses were initiated: rapid breathing, increased heart rate, accelerated biochemical/hormone secretions to improve performance, muscle tension, increased blood pressure, increased body temperature and consequent perspiration to cool the body so it ran efficiently. So through physical changes you learn to recognise feeling afraid or angry. These body changes also provide an influx of energy to fight the threat, or to run away from it.

These days, bears and tigers can take the form of your boss criticising you, other road-users, jobs required 'yesterday', technology that has broken down, in fact any threat to your job, status, personal worth or physical wellbeing. These are often called stressors. The problem is, like the threats to your ancestors, these modern-day threats produce the same automatic responses in your body. They are, however, only as useful as they once were—for short periods of actual physical threat, such as crossing the road.

Usually, the threats you perceive these days are not violent, although they may be experienced frequently. Because the emotional body responses are produced for relatively longer periods of time, the consequences can be damaging. You do not often run for your life out of your office or factory, nor do you usually have a physical fight with the supervisor who has just told you that you aren't worth your wages. You do not actually need the extra energy, muscle tension, or other body changes. So when you are threatened you are like a car in gear with the engine accelerating, but with every available brake applied. It is not difficult to imagine how a car in this situation might start to shake and shudder and that after a while some of the bits might start to fall off.

Effects of fright (without flight or fight)

Several other responses that occur when you are threatened are worth noting:

- Blood-clotting ability increases in preparation for possible injury.
- The liver releases sugar, cholesterol and fatty acids into the blood for quick energy.
- Immune responses temporarily decrease. This change allows your body to respond faster and more vigorously.

It is well recognised that prolonged body tension decreases your capacity to function. It has become part of everyday language. People talk about being stressed out or burnt out. Extreme or continued threat (producing stress or tension) can be seen as a cause, or at least a contributor, to emotional breakdown. Diagnosed anxiety and depressive conditions, as well as normal fear and anger, can be partly attributed to our body's response to stressors.

If you are tense in your body you will be tense in your mind; if you are tense in your mind you will be tense in your body.

There is a close interaction between what you feel in your body and what you experience in your mind. If your body is reacting in a threatened way it is telling you that you ought to be doing something, that you ought to be worried. Conversely, if you identify something as threatening you are likely to get your body aroused with all the responses that have been described.

Consequences of prolonged body tension

Apart from psychological disturbance there are other probable consequences of prolonged body reactions. These include the obvious and likely results of muscle tension such as discomfort in your shoulders or in your jaws caused by teeth grinding—a body tension response which can continue in sleep. Less obvious is the effect on your immune system.

The immune system controls your body's responses to attacks from outside, such as infections. It assists your recovery when you break an arm or when something causes you to produce a defective cell that needs to be prevented from growing. In everyday life, you perhaps recognise this when you say someone is run down, that is, they have been experiencing stress, and because of this they caught a cold or got the flu.

If you are tense in your body you will be tense in your mind; if you are tense in your mind you will be tense in your body.

It is generally well-recognised that continued stress responses weaken the immune system. If immune system responses themselves are low then a body climate is created that is more likely to permit the onset of illness.

Sometimes the connection between the stress and the person's response, and something going wrong with your body is not easily shown. To trace a condition like cancer to a single cause like stress is almost certainly going to be misleading, since it is likely that there are a range of other contributing factors. It is nonetheless commonly accepted that stress is a contributor to stomach ulcers and can be a factor in heart attacks.

For the purposes of this book we need conclude only that your body reactions to threat can contribute to both psychological and medical problems and are a source of discomfort. What you need to be able to do is to note the beginnings of feeling afraid or angry and be able to do something about it.

It is important to note that the flight/fight response, which these days is often called the *stress response*, is something that is taking place inside you. Threats to your security and your aspirations produce these body responses (feelings), which in turn lead your physical system into tension and stress.

A stressor for one person may not be a stressor for another. Being criticised on a personal level—being told you are mean, lazy or ugly, can be a bother for some people, but not to others; driving a car can be relaxing for some people, but produces fear and anxiety (tension) in others. It depends on what *you see* as a threat. The same snake may terrify one person but not another; the other person may either know that the snake is not venomous, or has, perhaps because of experience, confidence in his or her ability to handle the situation. The same is true for threats in work situations, at home or in general living. What produces anger or fear for one person won't for another. For one person the boss's criticisms are like water off a duck's back; another takes the same criticisms to heart.

Of course, not all these emotional feelings are bad for you. You may sometimes need a little bit of nervous energy to improve your performance. Being too laid back for that job interview may mean that you do not prepare properly. Actors before going on stage may be nervous which, if not too distressing, can improve their performance. Similarly, athletes need the extra adrenalin to produce their best results. The deliberate tension induced by various forms of 'psyching up' in sport is another form of positive stress—the haka performed by New Zealand rugby players is a spectacular example.

If you notice the feelings you are experiencing and can recognise enabling ones and know how to manage the others, then they are not undermining your short-term happiness by causing distress, or longer-term happiness in the form of ill-health. You need to learn when you are starting to feel stressed and conversely what it feels like to feel calm.

Relaxed, calm and cool

While it is clear that our ancestors used their threat/fright body responses to increase their chances of survival, it is also probable that this rush of energy stopped when they were safe from predators and other threats. They relaxed. The *relaxation response* is the very opposite of the stress response. The internal activity of the body is reduced and the automatic functions are calmer. To say 'it's cool' does have physiological meaning—when you are in a relaxed state, the system is not so heated—blood pressure is lower, heart rate slows, and temperature of the brain is slightly lower.

The way to reduce stress and improve comfort is to produce the relaxation response. If you are relaxed in your body you will be relaxed in you mind; if you are relaxed in your mind you will be relaxed in your body.

To stop feverish mental activity is a goal often difficult to achieve: it can be easier to focus on ways of relaxing your body. If you relax your body it will help your mind to relax as well.

Listening to your body talk

One of the difficulties you may sometimes experience is knowing when you are tense. It can be that only *after* experiencing jaw pain that you recognise you have been tensing your jaw or grinding your teeth. It may be that only when you are half-way home from work that you notice you are clenching the steering wheel. It may be only after periods of prolonged body tension that you notice that ache across your shoulders.

If you gather information about what you are doing—become aware—you will probably adjust in some way. A person born blind who gains sight as an adult may take as long as several months to actually see properly. The brain has to adjust to what the body is seeing before it can put it all together and see normally. This process of getting new information and adjusting to it is called feedback—something to which we all respond. One of the best ways to get tennis players to improve their serve, for example, is to show them an immediate video replay of it.

So a key part of learning to relax is being able to recognise when you are tense. In the last twenty-five years, *biofeedback* has become a tool of the helping professions. Biofeedback refers to the methods that can be used to help you to 'hear or see' what your body is 'telling

The way to reduce stress and improve comfort is to produce the relaxation response.

or showing' you. Some of this is technical. There are machines that can show changes to the amount of sweat being secreted on the palms of your hands; machines that can measure muscle tension in certain parts of your body; machines that can plot your brainwave patterns. Such machines are used by some therapists to teach an individual person their own body talk, and thus help them recognise when they may need to do something to adjust their stress/tension levels.

There are some other technical but less machine-driven means that you can use to help you know what is happening in your body, such as taking your own heart (pulse) rate. Some of the less expensive kinds of machines are also becoming commercially available.

Fortunately there are other ways you can also learn (or relearn) to recognise some of your own body responses. By pausing and paying careful attention to what you are experiencing, you may, for example, learn to recognise when there are changes to your level of excitement, your heart rate, your muscle tension, or, if you become very observant, changes to your body temperature. Through these means, even without the extra benefit of machines, you can give yourself some biofeedback.

Biofeedback can be positive or negative. In sport, for example, there are times when you know you have got some play just right—you can feel it. On the other hand, there are situations when you can notice your muscle tension increasing. The task is to become more skilful at recognising your body talk and then to be able to bring on the relaxation response if it is needed.

One of the skills you may need to learn, if you do not already have it, is how to notice when you have body tension. It sounds too easy to say *pay attention to your body*, but this is a key way to recognise your body tension. Mostly probably you do not pay attention to your body unless it is *demanding* attention, such as if you are in pain or desperately want to go to the loo.

Exercise 7: Recognising body tension

Stop for a minute or two, say three or four times in a day, and do a body check:

- Am I feeling tension in my shoulders, jaw, hands or legs?
- Am I raising my shoulders and breathing quickly into my upper chest, or am I breathing in a more relaxed fashion with my body erect but my shoulders lowered (not bent over)?

While you need to know what it feels like to be tense, it is also necessary to learn what it feels like to be relaxed. You may think you are relaxed, for example, watching television, but if you attend to your body you may find some of your muscles still tense, perhaps a carry-over from your work experiences on that day.

One way of knowing what it feels like to have the relaxation response is to engage in an activity which will bring it on.

Ways of producing the relaxation response

There are dozens of ways that people can learn to feel the relaxation response. Libraries have books on the topic; you can hire or buy tapes of relaxing or soothing music; read ways of using your imagination to help you feel calm; you could have a massage.

It is worth remembering that if, for example, you induce one aspect of the relaxation response, such as relaxing the muscles of your body, other aspects of the relaxation response are also likely to be triggered, such as lowering your blood pressure. With relaxation comes increased *comfort*.

Two slightly different but well-known ways of relaxing are given below. The first important result is for your mind and your body to learn, and remember, what the relaxation response feels like, so that you can bring it on when you want to. If you decide to try one of these approaches, it is probably best if you stick to just one of them for at least a few weeks.

Exercise 8: Progressive muscle relaxation

Progressive muscle relaxation is one of the most common ways of producing the relaxation response. You may have already experienced it or heard of it. It has the advantage of helping the person using it to recognise the feelings of tension and relaxation and to notice the difference.

- Ensure that your clothes are loose-fitting. Take your shoes off if that feels more comfortable.
- Choose a comfortable sitting or reclining position. You can begin muscle relaxation starting at your feet and moving progressively up your body to your head, or vice versa. We begin with your feet.
- Now, feel your toes—the balls of your feet—the whole of your feet.
- Tense up your toes; make them tight—tense up the rest of your feet.
- Pause and notice what you feel; hold it a little while—release it.
- Now let the muscles of your toes relax, go loose, feel comfortable—now let the rest of your feet relax—notice what you feel.
- Feel your ankles—your shins—and calf muscles.
- Tense up your ankles, make them tight—tense up your shins and tense up, tighten, your calf muscles.
- Pause and hold it a little while—notice what you feel.
- Relax your ankles—relax your shins—relax/loosen your calf muscles.
- Notice what you feel.

Continue this process, focusing on the particular parts of the body: tense them up; notice what that feels like; relax them, and notice what that feels like. Move through knees and thighs; base of the spine and pelvic area; lower back and lower stomach; middle back and upper stomach; upper back and chest; fingers and hands; forearms; upper arms; shoulders; muscles of the neck; jaw and muscles of the cheek; muscles around the eyes and forehead.

You may find it easier to ask a friend to read these steps to you. They would need to go slowly with plenty of lengthy, several second pauses where the dashes are shown. Repeat the words for each part of the body. Similarly, you could yourself record these steps on an audio tape and play them at a suitable time. The whole process should take approximately ten to fifteen minutes.

The point is to learn to feel the relaxation response, to notice it, to remember the feeling and to use it in the future.

Exercise 9: Stomach breathing

Stomach breathing, or as it is more formally known, *abdominal breathing*, has come into use in recent years as a means of managing panic attacks. While it is clearly important for that purpose, it has been my experience that it is also a useful relaxation strategy.

Research has shown that when some people get anxious they breathe rapidly into their upper chest, and this changes the acid level of their blood, which in turn can cause a range of different body responses such as increased perspiration, tremors, feeling nauseous and feeling that their heart is racing. These body feelings make the person more anxious and so produce more of that kind of breathing with the consequent body feelings.

Abdominal breathing has been used as a way of interrupting this cycle and controlling these distressing feelings. While you may not experience panic attacks, you may find the technique useful for general relaxation. Once learnt, it can be done in just a few minutes.

- Start by sitting in front of a mirror so that you can see your chest and your stomach clearly.
- Sit erect, but let your shoulders drop on each side; do not hold your upper body tense.
- Breathe in at a natural (not forced) pace. Don't worry whether you are breathing through your nose or your mouth.
- Breathe into your stomach. If you hold your hand on your stomach you may notice it rise slightly. It is important to note that your shoulders are not raised while you are breathing in and that breathing in is not forced.

- The pace is normal (which can seem slow sometimes); a breath is once in and out; you should be taking about seven breaths a minute.
- Breathe in this way for a couple of minutes. It is the kind of natural breathing you may see a young baby do. It is not forced deep breathing.

Once you have learnt to do this you can pause during the day for a minute or two and practise it—if you are self-conscious, in front of other people, you can practise it when you go to the toilet!

Bill's story: Living calmly

Bill had been appointed manager of a large nursing home. He had come from another city and was not known to the staff of the home—many of whom had been employed there for quite some time. In his first 18 months of employment, he developed angina symptoms. After medical investigation it was decided to operate and provide Bill with a double by-pass. He returned to work after the usual convalescent period. It was shortly after this that Bill's doctor suggested he see me with a view to improving his emotional reactions to his work. It was hoped that such an improvement may contribute to a reduction in his high blood pressure.

After discussion it became clear that Bill was reacting, as anyone might, to the obstructive techniques some of the entrenched staff were using. This included not completing roster details, not passing on messages, fighting with other staff about shift change-over times and complaining to Board members about efficiency improvements being proposed by Bill.

During our sessions Bill developed an approach that included reshaping the way he saw the other staff—they were no longer the enemy—rather they were frightened and afraid themselves. Similarly he rehearsed with his wife strategies for managing these people, such as taking one step at a time and ensuring communications were clear and sometimes written.

A main feature of his own health management was learning relaxation methods that included progressive muscle relaxation and listening to calming music. I also think, in his case, that the occasional game of golf was helpful.

Several years have elapsed since this time and although he has changed jobs, which was probably wise, Bill remains in a good state of health and continues to practise his relaxation techniques.

Excitement

Excitement is another raw emotion, along with fear and anger, which you often feel in the pit of your stomach. The adrenalin rush of the rollercoaster is not for everyone though undoubtedly some of us enjoy those feelings bordering on the edge of fear. The absence of real physical threats in our lives may motivate us to seek out experiences, often imagined, as in adventure or horror movies, which will safely frighten us.

It is very much an individual matter. I once had a relative who would not go to football matches because he was frightened the excitement would give him a heart attack. For others sporting events are no more exciting than watching the grass grow.

Absolutely everyone needs a little excitement in their lives. Whether you get this in your work, or vicariously by reading a book or watching a film, or through more direct involvement in bowls, sky-diving, mountain climbing, trekking, or fishing is an individual matter.

Are you aware of feelings of excitement in your life? You need to be sure that they fit your happiness goals. There are people who enjoy the feelings of excitement they experience from driving dangerously fast. Is this you?

Of course, excitement at work, at home or on the sporting field can bring you anger, frustration and extra stress that is obviously not beneficial. Even the feeling of being hyped-up for a few months with arrangements for a special event such as a wedding anniversary or a trip away can undermine your happiness. The key is maintaining balance by undertaking some relaxing and calming activities every day.

REFLECTION

During the next week notice how you are getting your adrenalin rushes. Are they from activities which do you no harm and may even do you some good? If not, what other ways can you satisfy your excitement needs?

Knowing intuitively

The other major way of trusting your feelings is to be able to recognise your intuitive knowledge.

You have probably had experiences where you feel confident that you know something to be true. Perhaps it is about another person, a house you are looking to buy, or an outing that you are planning. It may be that you feel good or bad vibes. Sometimes you may have ignored such feelings only to find out later that they were correct.

The exercises in this chapter will help you to develop ways of calling upon this wisdom. The first step is to help you develop, or resurrect, your visualisation skills. The second is to use these abilities to harness your intuitive knowledge. The creative power of dreaming as a source of wisdom is also considered.

Visualisation

Have you seen a tennis player adjust the strings of their racket in between receiving serves? They are often trying to use this to recall a visual memory and a body feeling of how they make good returning shots. Visualising situations, including imaginary ones, is a creative capacity that can enhance not only the performance of the artist or the dancer, but can also help you improve your performances and give you access to knowledge of which you are sometimes unaware.

The following exercise gives you an opportunity to re-experience visualising, which is something you have probably done many times. Its purpose is to provide a base exercise to which other steps can be added. While the first approach uses guided imagery, that is the 'pictures' to imagine are suggested to you, you may find after you have done it that you would prefer to make up your own imaginary setting; a second approach is given in the exercise to help you do this also.

Visualising situations, including imaginary ones, is a creative capacity that can enhance not only the performance of the artist or the dancer, but can also help you improve your performances and give you access to knowledge of which you are sometimes unaware.

Exercise 10: A safe place

The inner projection of a safe place is a common imaginary exercise.

First steps:

- Make a tape of the script below or have a friend available to read it.
- Make yourself comfortable—lying down or sitting in an easy chair.
- Close your eyes—though you can visualise with your eyes open it is generally easier to do, at least initially, with your eyes closed.
- Suspend your critical abilities. Some people say that they put their 'inner critic' on hold. By which they mean that they are avoiding logical analysis, or self-criticism.
- Relax by any means already suggested. For many people, just breathing slowly and evenly is sufficient.

Guided script:

(The script should be read very slowly and evenly, with a calm voice and with plenty of pauses; anything from ten to thirty seconds a pause is okay. You can also add pauses to the ones shown in the script. The whole script can last from five to fifteen minutes.)

As you breathe evenly and deeply you can take yourself to a safe, pleasant beach—while you are there you can see the gentle waves lapping the edge of the shore—the gulls flying overhead—you can see just a few clouds in an otherwise blue sky through which the sun shines—as you see these things you can feel the warmth of the sun gently on your back—and—the warm sand underneath your feet, slipping between your toes as you walk—after a while—you choose a place to sit—as you sit down you note the texture of the sand and the occasional piece of sea-weed—you can smell the sea salt—you can feel a gentle breeze in your face—overhead you hear one or two gulls calling out—all these experiences help you to feel calm, comfortable and at ease—you can pause for a while here and enjoy these feelings.

After you have rested for a while you can take three deep breaths and return to this room (or wherever you are).

For some people a directed or guided approach such as the one above is not as acceptable as a self-directed form of imagining. For this reason, a sample script in which you provide the detail is now given. As with the guided script in which the imagery was guided, making a tape for yourself or having someone take you through it is likely to be the most helpful way to use it.

Self-directed script:
(Go through the first steps on page 93. Again use plenty of pauses.)

As you breathe evenly and deeply you can get yourself as comfortable as possible—and when you are ready you can take yourself to a pleasant, safe, secure place—it can be a real or imaginary place, it can be inside or outdoors, whatever you choose—a place where you feel comfortable and calm and in control—when you get there, enjoy it—while you are there you can notice the shapes of the things around you—take your time to do this—look around and see what is there—notice the colours of these objects—perhaps you can sit or lie down there—and when you do, feel the texture of the surface on which you are sitting or lying—as you feel these things you become even more absorbed in your surroundings—you can perhaps even notice some pleasant sounds which add to

the relaxing character of your safe, secure place—some people recog-
nise friendly smells which are associated with their special place—once
again pause and enjoy it—when you are ready you can take three deep
breaths and, taking all the time that you need, return to this room (or
wherever you are).

Once you have designed your own special place you can use it over and over, although occasionally you may want a change and go somewhere else, and that's fine.

The more you practise visualisation exercises the better able you will be to apply them. Even at the introductory level described above they can become a source of increased peace and comfort and heightened imagination. These safe place exercises also provide a visual imagery base to which can be added other visualisations.

Getting messages from your unconscious
Many teachers of visualisation talk about *inner guides* or *wise persons*. Another way of picturing your inner guide is as a *personal inner adviser* who, in business language, acts as a consultant to you. What happens is that there is a part of your brain which relies on pictures, stories, symbols and wholistic understanding to communicate. You can think of your inner adviser as a way of getting advice from this part of your brain. Just as in art, or in children's art, or in art therapy, a drawing may convey the meaning of some unconscious message. The inner adviser provides a source of wisdom not generally consciously available to us. This advice is still part of you, but in a form that you do not always tap, as most often you are centred on your conscious thoughts, your logical and reasoning way of thinking.

When you begin to visualise your personal adviser, you naturally need to settle on an appropriate image. He or she might be a wise old man or woman, a *teacher*, such as a monk, or a person from a different cultural tradition. He or she could be someone you know or have met, someone from a film or story or legend or history, even an animal. The main thing is that they can reach useful conclusions and decisions without going through the step-by-step process you generally use in reasoning things out.

The answers they provide to your questions may not always be in a direct form. You could ask about applying for a particular job. In your mind you should frame the question with the meaning, 'Would it be a suitable kind of job for me?' Not, 'Am I going to get it?' Your personal adviser cannot know that! And the response may be to show you a picture of a different building, or a scene of you talking, in a work context, with someone you have never met (in other words *go for it*). Alternatively you may hear some discordant music as a response, or see someone swimming for their life (in other words *forget it*).

Once you have designed your own special place you can use it over and over, although occasionally you may want a change and go somewhere else, and that's fine.

Your questions may be answered in the form of pictures or scenes, or in symbols. In the example above, a positive symbol would be the adviser giving you a new bag or a new tie or a new brooch, or, straightforwardly a simple nod of the head, or a smile. Ambiguous or difficult-to-understand answers, or a shrug of the shoulders, may simply be meant to convey that now is not the time to have an answer. These intuitive responses to your questions are based on what that part of your brain knows about you. It is worth remembering that a humorous response can also be a creative answer to your question.

Exercise 11: Contacting your personal adviser (consultant)

Start by going through one of the two earlier visualisation exercises (pages 93–5) then follow this visualisation sequence in which you provide the detail:

Once you are comfortable in your safe, secure place, imagine you can see a figure in the distance which gets larger as it comes closer, and, as it does, its shape becomes more clearly visible. If it is a person, notice what they are wearing and as they get closer observe the features of face, hair, eyes, nose and shape of mouth. If the person or creature seems unfriendly or dangerous do not invite them into your safe place. Have them turn around and go back the way they came, disappearing into the distance. In any case you only invite someone or some creature into your safe place after you have confirmed that they are your adviser (by, for example, asking them and getting a positive answer). If the answer is no or ambiguous, ask them to go away and send you your adviser.

When your friendly person or creature is with you in your safe place, show them around, go for a walk, point out things of interest and generally interact in a friendly way. When it is time for the adviser to go, say that you will keep in touch. Promise to invite them to return in a few days. Finish off in the same way as you did for the other visualisations, spending a little time alone in your special place before you return to other activities.

In a few days, return to this visualisation sequence, perhaps with a question for your adviser. Your questions can relate to any area of your life, but anything about your personal resources—relationships, new enterprises or lifestyle issues— are likely to be most fruitful and have a direct bearing on your happiness goals.

Dreaming—a case of involuntary intuition?

There are dreams that are obviously dependent on your physical state. I can remember, as a teenager, dreaming I was eating a small cream-cake with a caterpillar on top of it. Needless to say I woke feeling violently nauseous! Most probably you will have dreams where you want to urinate, or are thirsty, hungry or sexually aroused.

Similarly, you can have dreams in response to your

emotional state. In these you may imagine interacting in a distressing way at work, home or in a social situation. Perhaps you are running away, having an argument, being criticised or reliving a past problem such as doing again that job you hated. It is not difficult to recognise the meaning of these dreams.

People who have had a traumatic experience, as a result of being attacked, or being in a war, or being tortured, or being in an accident, may have nightmares related to their experience, even years later.

There are, however, some dreams that give you messages about your life in pictures, little stories and symbols, just like your inner adviser. If you can capture these, then you may learn creative advice that will help you live more consistently with your happiness goals.

Some people say they never dream. What is most likely is that they do not remember them.

TIPS

- Take your time rising in the morning, rather than getting out of bed in the style of a startled cat. Let yourself wake up naturally.
- Expect to find the dreams of some use to you. Remind yourself from time-to-time that you will probably start recalling more dreams (but don't try to force this).
- When you awake from a dream, relax and let yourself remember it and then make a note of it on the pad you have beside your bed.
- Watch less television at night.
- Talk with others about your dreams.
- Review your dream for its message content. While some may be obtuse, remember that the messages will commonly be in picture form or symbols, and will often be as easy to interpret as ones from your inner adviser.
- If you have a problem, 'sleep on it'; let your creative brain do its work unconsciously and tell you its result later.

Summary

You have learnt:

- the origin of gut feelings such as fear and anger, and their negative emotional effects in your life.
- the importance of recognising your feelings, including ways of noticing stress and relaxation responses.
- how to produce the relaxation response.
- the positive and negative value of excitement.
- the role of intuitive knowledge in seeking happiness. How to access this wisdom including using your personal adviser.
- the potential usefulness of understanding your dreams.

Managing stress can mean you need to increase your feelings of personal worth. Some strategies you may need to build your self-esteem are suggested in the next chapter. You may need, for example, to convince yourself that your performance is as good as others in sport, work or recreation, or that you are doing jobs around the house as well as you can, or that you can learn this computer application, and so on.

PRINCIPLE 3
IT IS BETTER TO SERVE YOURSELF THAN YOUR EGO

To serve your ego is often to direct your attention to others by doing things to get their recognition through such means as exercising control over them, or by seeking to participate in high-status activities or positions.

To serve yourself, on the other hand, is to take action through word, deed or thought to improve your self-esteem. It is about accurately recognising your own worth; knowing who you are, and, in particular, your good qualities and abilities. Your attention is directed inward.

In this section, managing those ego-goals that may impede your progress is what we look at first. This is followed by looking at ways you can fully understand yourself and recognise your own worth. Like your beliefs about your personal worth, your ego-goals have been learnt.

Ego-goals

Some of those ego-goals that can become a problem in life are actually generally held views, often reflected in the media.

Power/status
A plethora of stories in the media focus on the importance of power. An awful lot of time is given to larger-than-life heroes.

It is not only under-ten-year-olds that go to see *Superman* or *Batman and Robin*! In films, comics, books, magazines, television, radio, in songs and computer games, status and power is shown as valuable. In Batman's case, and in the real world, considerable financial backing supports these values.

Power is very much part of your real life. The news media and popular magazines, too, cultivate your interest in the rich and powerful to sell their products by producing stories on the lives of high-status people.

So, we are bombarded with messages about the desirability of power and wealth. But the truth of this message is not the issue. It is not whether getting wealth gives you power—it probably does—but whether the power once achieved brings you happiness. It is more a question of relevance. Being extra tall might be a good thing for your life if you play basketball for the Chicago Bulls, but if you don't, being extra tall could be a handicap.

Lottery winners who become millionaires overnight can strike trouble if they depart too rapidly from their regular lives. The ones who seem to cope most successfully with newly acquired wealth are those who continue many of their normal living routines.

Showing powerful characters as vulnerable is acceptable and probably desirable. Nevertheless it is important to recognise that the effect of power is dependent on circumstances. Financial independence can be empowering, enabling a person to exercise greater control over their life. The feelings of self-worth of many women, for example, have been increased by better access to employment and income.

> **We are bombarded with messages about the desirability of power and wealth. But the truth of this message is not the issue. It is not whether getting wealth gives you power—it probably does—but whether the power once achieved brings you happiness.**

Goals such as power can either contribute to or diminish your feelings of happiness. It depends what the power is used for—to control others, to indulge or distract yourself on the one hand, or to support others, or engage in creative pursuits, on the other.

Right is might?

You may have been taught that success invariably comes to people who are morally 'good'. There are some religious organisations that support this view. It is a theme taken up in very many movie genres. It is a message we learn well. Many of us are terribly disappointed with stories and films where the good do not win!

Being right is often not enough. In fact, sometimes it can lead you down an extremely distressing path of anger and recrimination.

While in life the good may sometimes win, it is not a universal truth, and to think it is may lead you down an ill-considered path, even in the short term. One automobile association used to talk about drivers who died maintaining their right of way. It is worthwhile wondering who is happy in a state of road rage—the one raging or the one raged against?

Probably neither! However, the raging driver is almost definitely a person who will often find themselves dissatisfied with life's circumstances because life presents many situations that cannot be controlled. Their unhappiness comes from their demanding ego-goals: 'I must be able to do what I want on the road without others interfering.'

Being right is often not enough. In fact, sometimes it can lead you down an extremely distressing path of anger and recrimination. Indeed, asserting your righteousness is often another way of trying to exercise power.

REFLECTION

The question for you is: what part does status and power play in your happiness? Do you strongly desire status and power? Are you happy with your position in life? It may help you to look away from status and power goals and focus on what really matters to you. Go back to Exercise 2, page 40. If you have put control goals on the top of your list, you may ask yourself what you are going to do with them?

The other side of power

The other side of power, control and influence is charity, compassion and acceptance. While these different, people-directed non-ego goals can lead to increased happiness, they are not big in the media even though they are occasionally portrayed there. Mother Teresa may have been shown as a wonderful person but not as a role model, whereas well-known actors, rock stars and high achievers in sport are often shown as people to emulate. It would seem strange to imagine the Pope, the Dalai Lama or Mother Teresa, if she were alive, promoting NutriGrain® or Weetabix®.

Perhaps you can't be a saint but you can be an ordinary person, so you may think, and so you are told. Despite this, more happiness pay-offs may come from pursuing goals focused on compassion and consideration, rather than the kind of power which has as its objective directly controlling others. Indeed exercising compassion can result in increased influence on others (a kind of indirect control). By listening to that person's problem you may not only assist them, but encourage them to share their thoughts with you in the future.

Control

The *control* goal was given as part of the definition of happiness at the start of this book. However, it is the control over your own life rather than the lives of others that is likely to bring you most joy. *Control* through influence is less likely to be damaging to you than *control* through the exercise of power.

Sometimes, too, it is a mistake to think that your future is controlled by your personal actions.

FOR EXAMPLE

What if:

• Hitler's mother had been driving to a liaison with Hitler's prospective father and a dog running across the road had caused her to have an accident and as a consequence Hitler was not born? Has the dog changed the course of history?

• Or, more personally, you actually got that job you applied for? Would it have made you happy or given you more problems?

• Or you didn't go to that rock concert and meet that special person? Your life might have been very different.

Your life can be influenced by a wide variety of possibilities. Although you are not in sole control of life's circumstances, you can exercise some control over how you feel and think.

Immediate satisfaction

Independent and immediate action by an individual is often something strongly and publicly advocated. This is reflected in the just-do-it approach. These people believe that too much analysis before action may be inhibiting.

FOR EXAMPLE

An athlete who was asked the secret of his success said, 'Man, when I get out of them blocks, I just run like hell!'

Nevertheless the idea that you will find happiness through solo self-seeking action is at least partially misleading. Much of your personal success and the achievement of your goals comes from your interaction with others and from the clarity of your short- and long-term planning. This runs counter to obeying your impulses. Most successful people plan and remain focused on their plans and are not often distracted by the prospect of immediate gratification.

Money, money, money

Money and happiness are quite possibly linked in your mind and in your actions. The media, almost to the last piece of celluloid, video tape or drop of ink seem to equate the accumulation of money as highly important to how you feel. To obtain more money than you presently have is almost uniformly put forward as a happiness goal.

In current affairs shows, decreased taxes and increased wages are invariably reported as desirable goals. Financial success appears more valued, more prominently treated than most other kinds of success. You may even find you have a sneaking admiration for the rather nasty 1980s corporate film character, played by actor Michael Douglas, who said that 'greed is good'. The problem is that the message is mixed. As noted earlier, more money will buy you more comfort and control (freedom to travel or to be less reliant on others, for example). It will not generally solve life's problems or consistently provide long-term comfort.

How you obtain additional spending power and what you do with it is also critical. You can be unhappy on a holiday. Many people are! A simple, relaxing and recreational country holiday may be much more satisfying than a luxury cruise.

The difficulty is that financial success is given an importance in both fictional and news media in excess of the role it actually plays. Your view of its importance is encouraged in lottery advertisements with the message 'I want to break free'; in election campaigns with promises of more income, less taxes and more facilities; in get-rich-quick books; and in regular articles on money matters in newspapers, which by their mere presence, even if you don't read them, tell you how important money is. Money is important, but perhaps not as important as you may have been led to believe. It can even work against you if it diminishes the value of your other happiness goals or limits their achievement. For example, you may spend too much of your time thinking about, or acting on, the financial aspects of your life, such as, focusing on getting the next better paying job, continually doing overtime, or skimping on food and outings so as to save more.

The most constructive action you can take is to manage your ego-goals (power, status, money, self-righteousness, gratification) in suitable ways. It is also necessary to make the most of yourself. You need to:

- understand how you see yourself (so that you recognise what might need adjusting to focus more on personal rather than ego-goals).
- learn how to straighten out any crooked thinking you may have about yourself (so that you can focus more on your needs).
- find ways of establishing a helpful but accurate 'self-story' which you can live by (thus improving how you feel).

Self-awareness

The human mind has the ability to be reflective, to be aware of its own thoughts and to speculate on the thoughts of others. Self-description is part of this self-awareness. It is probably a major influence on your life and your capacity to get what you want.

Exercise 12: How do you see yourself?

1. What are the things you do best? Examples: paint a picture, drive a bus, fix a car, play tennis.

_____

_____

_____

2. On what topics or subjects are you most knowledgeable? If you had to be on a quiz show, what topics would you nominate to be asked questions about?

(Knowledge topics need not be the same as the activities in which you think you are skilful. For example, you could be a skilful home gardener but most knowledgeable about Olympic swimming champions, history of World War II or Australian wines.)

_____

_____

_____

3. Use three words to describe how you relate to other people. Examples: confronting, relaxed and open, shy, with humour.

_____

_____

_____

4. Imagine you are asked to introduce yourself to a new group of people in a recreational setting. What would you say? Examples: 'I am married with three children and I'm good at sports', or 'I like fishing and buying smart clothes'.

_____

_____

_____

5. What would you keep back (i.e. things about yourself that you would not want other people to know about)? Examples: 'I have fantasies about beating up the boss', 'I would not want people to know that I applied twice for that job and didn't get it', 'I don't think my husband loves me'.

_____

_____

_____

6. If you were introducing yourself to a new work or training group, would you share or keep back the same description of yourself as you would do with a recreational group? Write down any parts of your self-description that may vary. Example: I might talk about my mechanical, culinary or other skills, or about my previous workplace.

_____

_____

_____

Using the results of Exercise 12

This exercise did not ask you directly to focus on negative aspects of your self-description, although these also form part of how you think about yourself. Your capacity to reach your happiness goals is substantially dependent on the strength of your positive self-beliefs, as every motivational speaker will testify. If your negative self-assessments are not strong (e.g. you may see yourself as not being a particularly good cook, while also feeling cooking isn't overly important to you), or lack relevance (e.g. you might think you are not good at learning foreign languages, but know that this negative self-view doesn't affect your daily living), they will not detract significantly from your achieving your happiness goals.

If, on the other hand, you generally have poor self-esteem about, say, your popularity or your abilities, it may cause you to feel substantial emotional distress. If this happens, your thoughts are preventing you from experiencing comfort, control or creativity, even when to all appearances these happiness goals seem within your grasp. You may, for example, be so worried about giving a speech at a wedding reception that you cannot sit down and enjoy your favourite television programme. While this book looks at ways of managing negative self-views, the actual contribution of self-awareness to the achievement of happiness stems from positive self-views.

The exercise above identifies what you think are your main personal features—the ones which you believe are most characteristic of you. These form your base of confidence. *You can use these skills, knowledge and personal qualities by participating in activities that make the most of them.* Look for opportunities in your current or new workplace, in your choice of recreational activities or clubs, or in retirement, to use your best attributes.

You may sometimes not recognise your strengths because you haven't become sufficiently aware of them, or you do not see them as strengths in the way that others do.

REFLECTION

You can investigate your self-awareness by asking, separately, a couple of trusted friends to tell you what they think are your best skills, abilities or personal attributes.

If you discover a new attribute in this way, you may need to remind yourself of it from time to time and consciously use this awareness in your choice of work tasks and recreational pursuits.

Part of evolving an accurate view of yourself is to remove incorrect, distorted or unreasonable views, not only of what you are like but also of what you *should* be like.

Straightening out crooked thinking

Sometimes you develop a distorted or twisted view of yourself, other people, and the world, and this produces what a well-known therapist, Albert Ellis, calls *irrational thinking*. This kind of thinking can lead you down a slippery path of guilt and blame, making you feel worried, uncomfortable and not in control of your life. Irrational ideas are often generalised ones, such as:

- All men are aggressive.
- All women have premenstrual tension.
- All politicians are 'on the take'.

You can also have irrational ideas about yourself such as:

- I must always do well or very well.
- I must never make a mistake.
- My life should be free of hassles.

These ideas can cause self-talk like: *If I am not performing perfectly then I am going to feel terrible* or *If that doesn't go right I am going to blow my stack* or *If I strike problems during the day I know I am just going to fall in a heap*. In other words your irrational belief about yourself or the world can place you in a position where, when things go wrong, as they sometimes will, you experience distressing emotions such as anxiety, depression or anger.

Ellis's recipe for straightening out this crooked thinking is to work out the irrational thought which is at the heart of your distress, to challenge it, and to dispute its reasoning.

Given the difficulty you may experience in changing your mind, even about your irrational beliefs, a sideways approach to this problem is to change *musts*, *oughts* and *shoulds* into preferences. For example, you could say: *I would prefer to do well*, rather than *I must* and therefore *It would be nice if I did well but I can cope if I don't*. This is a more rational way of thinking. It is a better reflection of the way things are. To follow this approach to improve the way you feel, it is necessary to practise this rational form of self-talk; after all, you may have had many years' experience in irrational self-talk.

Part of evolving an accurate view of yourself is to remove incorrect, distorted or unreasonable views, not only of what you are like but also of what you should be like.

Irrational thoughts can be about circumstances as well as about unreasonable self-expectations. They can be a belief that things in your life *should always* run smoothly, or that other people *should always* be reasonable, or that it is absolutely *impossible* for you to influence the way you feel, or that it is unfortunate circumstances and other people that *are responsible* for the way you feel.

Some of the hardest people to help are those who believe that the way they feel has nothing to do with what they do or think. It is every counsellor's nightmare—such people want you to fix the others (their boss, their partner or their children).

More commonly irrational thinking will diminish how you see yourself. In the following exercise, we learn how to turn around irrational thinking.

Exercise 13: Practising straighter thinking

1. As a first practice change into rational statements the irrational ones given below.

- *My life should always run smoothly.*
- *Other people should always be reasonable to me.*
- *It is impossible for me to change the way I feel.*
- *If it wasn't for what other people do to me and for what happens to me I would always feel fine.*

2. Find three situations in the last month where you have become angry or upset. Briefly write them down.

3. Work out what was the belief or the idea on which they were based. (It needs to be noted that some distressing experiences are not ordinarily thought of as irrational—such as the death of a loved one—though even here the extent to which you believe that this *should never* happen to you or that the other person *should always* be with you will affect the extent of your feelings of grief.)

4. Challenge and dispute the grounds of the irrational belief using the following questions, and make up your own questions.

- *Where is it written that I always must do well?*
- *Why must I be perfect?*
- *Who has said that I am a not a worthwhile person if I don't do well every time?*

5. Write out more rational, but still acceptable, statements. Rehearse these preferred statements and use them.

Jack's story: Straightening out his thoughts and feelings

Jack had worked for many years in the police force. He was considered a good officer, reliable, strong and able to relate exceptionally well to his local community. He had been in the district for many years and was well known there. He was a good father and loved his three children, supporting them in their sporting and school activities.

Throughout the period of his employment he was often the one given that extra tough job, such as telling parents of their son's suicide, without disclosing some of the more horrific details, or going to that accident scene where dismembered bodies created a rather gruesome picture. He didn't complain but often 'chilled out' in the police vehicle. Over the years these unexpressed feelings built up. Major changes started to happen in Jack's life after he was knocked back for a promotion. He felt it was unfair and became more and more distressed. He was on sick leave from work and, amongst other things, he barely left the house. If he did find himself in someone else's house, or, say, in a shop, he would stand with his back to the wall so that no one could approach him unexpectedly.

To improve how he felt Jack had to work through a number of issues relevant to this section of the book.

Jack's most pressing and immediate feelings concerned his perceptions that his superiors had abused their power. These feelings were not easily changed, but they diminished as he began to see the situation was not one he could readily control and as he recognised that there were more important things in his life (e.g. his family). He gradually recognised that his own ego-goals (for status and prestige) were making him feel worse. He also saw that some of his resentment was related to how he had been given hard jobs without much support. These experiences often caused him to feel inadequate as well as inwardly distressed.

Jack began a programme of recognising his personal worth— a goal supported by regular self-talk about his abilities and achievements. He also straightened out his crooked thinking. In the past, he always felt he had to be the strong, silent, macho type. This irrational view was challenged as he confronted rational questions such as: 'Why should I always be in control of my emotions? Where is it written that I must be able to help everyone?' and so on. In time, Jack was able to improve the way he felt.

He has now left the police force and runs his own small business, while leading a satisfying and fruitful family life.

Self-stories

Self-stories are the ones that you tell yourself. You've learnt them and recorded them in your mind. They are there for you to tune into at appropriate times, and they influence the way you feel. For our purposes a self-story can be quite short. It may be a family story about you that has been handed down by particular relatives. Other stories are based on your cultural background such as how a good wife or husband should behave, or what are acceptable ways of showing feelings, or whether an interest in sport or art is valued in your family. All these parts of your background may also influence your view of yourself.

One feature of self-stories especially pertinent to your happiness is that you also make them up about yourself. Perhaps your self-story is: *I am thorough and punctual*. You may use this very short description to build bigger stories. Thus in a family dispute about rubbish bins: *You know how thorough I am. There is no way that I wouldn't put the bin out at 7.30 the night before; that's what I always do.*

In a series of self-stories and descriptions about yourself and others you can write the story of your life. You may live by your stories. If you say: *I am a Libran; I can't stand a thing out of place*, you will become frustrated when things aren't tidy. To be more tolerant of disorder would require you to change, or to add to your self-descriptive story in some way that made untidiness more acceptable. Stories about how you should behave may cause you to behave sometimes in ways that are contrary to your long-term happiness.

FOR EXAMPLE

If you accept a story that says 'A real man can hold his drink', you could be placed in a position, as a male, of showing off your drinking prowess in the pub. Alternatively, as a female, if you accepted the same story, you may see a non-drinking male as not a 'real man'.

Perhaps to counteract this you could tell yourself another story. It's a favourite story for some people. Remember the fiercely physical comic-book character, the Phantom, who, as his other self, Mr Walker, only drank milk in bars!

Using stories to put your best foot forward

It is easy to use your natural tendency to tell and listen to stories to enhance your self-esteem in realistic ways.

Listen to helpful stories

Helpful stories are the ones that encourage you to act in ways which are more likely to achieve your happiness goals. You need to choose these stories carefully. This means checking out the messages of stories, explicit or hidden, in the songs, television and radio programmes you listen to, and the magazines and books you read.

You can actively seek out stories that you believe will help you live in a more *comfortable* (harmonious) and *creative* way.

- Read extracts from the various spiritual traditions.
- Choose to watch a television programme that is realistic and supports caring and sharing values.

- Read stories about people whose lives demonstrate the kind of values by which you want to live.
- Listen to folk songs that tell stories of endurance, perseverance and loyalty.
- Listen to motivational tapes made by successful individuals.

FOR EXAMPLE

A highly successful business woman attributes her success partly to the ten to twenty minutes she sets aside every day to read extracts of what could be called *uplifting* reading.

What is relevant for you is to find some time in the balance of your life to hear the helpful stories. If you frequently follow only the stories that support behaviour counter productive to your goals, it is not likely you will reach your happiness targets.

As well as stories that support your values it is important to hear and listen to positive stories about yourself. These will not only make you feel more comfortable, but will often lead you in more productive directions.

You need to seek out your supporters, to be with them, and hear them tell favourable stories about you.

Listening to destructive stories

'She never bothers with people she hates, that's why the lady is a tramp.' These words from the Rodgers and Hart song are good advice. In this song, a tramp is someone independent and free—someone to be admired. You probably have heard of, or experienced, family gatherings where one of the family is described as having certain attributes on which a set of stories are based.

FOR EXAMPLE

An example of a destructive story: 'You know Mary's asthma is a real problem for John (her husband) and their children.'

'Yes, I know. They would have gone for that holiday in the country, if he hadn't been worried about her allergies. It's the wildflowers you know.'

'And you know her children never go on a picnic for the same reason—it's a real shame.'

In this example, it is easy to imagine the implied responsibilities that would filter into conversations with Mary (e.g. to Mary: *It's a pity that your family holidays and outings are restricted by your asthma*). Mary is being led into a story where she is cast as the cause of some of her family's ills. Mary would be better off avoiding these large get-togethers and in this way limit the possibility of internalising destructive stories about herself. Additionally she may need to challenge, at least internally, the logic of these unreasonable stories.

While you may need accurate feedback about what you do, you have no need to listen to those who weave stories around you where you become responsible for other people's behaviour. You aren't responsible for their behaviour—they are.

Exercise 14: Writing your own script

1. One important way of changing the direction of your life is to start to rewrite your script. This may take place over a period of time. You need a small notebook for this exercise. Note the major stories and self-descriptions that surround your life. These are not only the stories that other people tell about you, but are also the things you say about yourself. The kinds of things you are listening for are statements that begin:

- *I like it when you*—(are generous; kind; help me with the ironing; share an outing together).
- *You know what they say about you*—(that you are never late; that you spend all your time on the computer).
- *I wish you wouldn't behave like a*—(fool; fuddy-duddy; restless twit).

Listen to things you say or think about yourself:

- *I know I can do that because—.*
- *I wish I was—.*
- *I am like a—.*

2. Record the stories, whether you like them or not. Just recognising them may have the effect of changing them.

3. After a month review the stories and put them into four categories:

a) Those you like and judge to be true. Hang on to these!

b) Those you like and are not sure if they are true. Ask yourself what would need to happen for you to believe these stories? What could you do that would help you believe these stories? For both categories a) and b) you need to check that the stories you like are also consistent with your happiness goals. The exercise assumes that those stories you dislike are not in your best interests. However, you may need to check this. If, for example, you don't like to be told it is unhealthy to smoke, you may need to take steps to change the story of yourself as a smoker.

c) Those you dislike and are not sure if they are true. What would you need to know to be assured that these stories were untrue? If they were true what do you need to do to make them untrue? Do you need help to do that? Where can you get this help?

d) Those you dislike and judge to be true. How can you change these stories? What help do you need? How will you know when the story has changed?

4. Use the notes you have made in answering these questions to make changes to your key stories. List three important changes.

_____

_____

_____

5. After another month check if you are using these revised stories. Review again. Make any further changes needed to improve your life script.

Matching your actions to your view

To be comfortable and at ease in your mind, your actions need to fit your views of yourself and the way you think things should be.

Poor matches

Behaviour that does not match your view of yourself will cause you unhappiness. At the worst extreme you may even reject accurate praise because it does not reflect how you see things. I have seen children with very poor self-esteem become angry and upset with what they judge to be excessive praise, because it did not match their poor opinion of themselves. They didn't trust the feedback.

> If you judge your actions to be inconsistent with how you see yourself, you are likely to feel guilty or upset. For instance, you may see yourself as a good listener and then notice yourself frequently interrupting another person's conversation.

Alternatively, if you judge your actions to be inconsistent with how you see yourself, you are likely to feel guilty or upset. For instance, you may see yourself as a good listener and then notice yourself frequently interrupting another person's conversation; you may think of yourself as a punctual person and then be terribly upset that you are running half an hour late for that meeting; or you may think of yourself as a good student and then be distraught because you've done poorly in an assignment.

If you are to be happy with your actions you need to be *congruent*. This word is used by psychologists and counsellors to refer to the way a therapist needs to interact with a client. In our context, it means being consistent. It means ensuring that your actions are consistent with your beliefs.

This advice is relevant to our daily living. Not following this advice is captured in the expression 'living a lie'. A commonly experienced example of this source of unhappiness is doing a job with which you disagree in principle. Exaggerated examples would include working at tree felling and logging while holding strong environmentalist beliefs, or taking the vow of celibacy as a Catholic priest and being sexually active.

It is less dramatic, but also disturbing, to behave in ways that don't match your beliefs about your roles (e.g. as a parent disciplining your child in a way which is different from your proclaimed views; as a tradesman pressed for time letting yourself do a sloppy job; as a bank officer approving a loan on which the customer is very likely to default).

Getting your actions and beliefs to match
To act or think in consistent ways you may need to reconsider your beliefs.

Some beliefs on child-rearing, for example, may be out of step with what is possible, or not applicable in all circumstances, or just plain wrong. On the other hand you may also need to be careful that you are not kidding yourself. If, for example, you talk about spending quality time with your children when in effect you just mean a little bit of time. Quality time may or may not mean more time. There is a difference between spending three hours with your child sitting in front of a television set and spending an hour interacting (playing a game, reading, or making something).

Similarly in the tree felling and logging example, your beliefs could be actually in tune with what seem to be conflicting actions. There may be environmental reasons for cutting down certain trees, or there may be no environmental harm in cutting down some trees and replanting others.

If, however, you deceive yourself with reasons that just help you feel more comfortable with your actions, then in the end you are likely to feel disturbed and unhappy.

FOR EXAMPLE
If you get yourself to believe that you are spending time with Grandma because you are a kind person, when in effect it (spending time with Grandma) is enabling you to get away from

your own children. If this in turn means leaving more of the child-rearing to your partner, then in time you may come to notice that your children lean on you less and less. You could be disappointed with that.

This is not about what is right or wrong, but about matching your actions with your values and self-beliefs.

Reconsider your behaviour

This may mean resigning from a job, seeking work in a different part of the enterprise or negotiating for less paid work time so that you can spend more time doing other activities that you also value, such as parenting, hobbies, sports, or community activities.

Sometimes (depending on the size of the organisation and the amount of energy you are prepared to spend) it may even be possible to work within an organisation to try and modify some of its approaches or goals to make them more consistent with those you value. Getting on that committee to promote more in-service training on, say, safety issues would be a good example.

Being genuine

Counsellors, in training, are often taught to be *authentic*. This refers particularly to establishing consistency between what you say and what you mean. If you are genuine in what you say then you are most likely being authentic.

When you have unhappiness which has at least in part been caused by dishonesty, distrust, distortion or secrecy, one way of trying to lose it is through being genuine. In practice this will mean:

- asking questions when you really don't understand.
- answering questions honestly yourself.

- being open, saying what you feel. This is sometimes called 'self-disclosing' and can mean sharing with suitable others your doubts, fears, feelings and aspirations.
- learning to trust others. Trusting someone else is a risk and sometimes people will betray this trust, but in most cases trust is repaid.

Summary

You have learnt that:

- devoting too much of your time to seeking power, status, prestige and money, for the largely ego-enhancing reasons of how others see you and what you can get from them, is likely to minimise rather than maximise happiness.
- happiness may come from avoiding ego-goals through the practice of compassion and consideration.
- self-awareness can contribute to your happiness objectives.
- a key part of self-awareness is learning methods for straightening out your crooked thinking.
- the role of the stories we tell ourselves (and our feelings of self-worth) can be enhanced by writing our own scripts.
- matching the way you act to the way you think is critical in serving yourself rather than your ego.

In the next chapter we look at how most forms of learning and creativity breed confidence and generate happiness.

PRINCIPLE 4
HAPPINESS IS GROWTH

One key ingredient of the happiness pie is growth in self-understanding and appreciation (Principle 3). The main focus of this section is growth as personal development. Growth can occur through:

- the way you think (growth in your mind).
- the tools you have available that help you remember and think.
- improving your communication with others.
- improving your creativity.

Growth in your mind

Concepts

Concepts are tools you use in your mind to help you learn. Conceptual or category thinking requires language and reflective thinking. An example would be: 'This type of seed can be ground up and used to make something to eat.' It is clear also that concepts are learnt from experience and opportunity. In other words, you would need to have the opportunity to recognise and distinguish one type of seed from another. The experience of watching others and participating enables you to learn how those seeds can be ground and made into flour and into dough and then cooked into something to eat.

There probably isn't a single person in today's world who could make a car from beginning to end. Who knows how to smelt the ore, *and* to make the metal, *and* to make the microchips, and to form the rubber? Most of us, however, have a basic idea, a *concept*, of how a car works, and you probably know when some parts of the car are not working. You have a concept of a working car which enables you to use the tool effectively and should you want to know more, say, about how tyres are made, you know where to go to get that information.

A concept is a tool which enables you to remember, understand and know how to do things without taking on board all the other details, the sheer volume of which you would find difficult to manage. Concepts can be ideas about how you should do something or about fields of learning. You can have concepts about fishing, language, building bridges or doing sums. They are the mental tools you use to help you achieve a desired result.

Concepts are mentally efficient. They save you thinking time. You don't have to learn with each lot of different ingredients how to make a curry. Once you've got the idea you can apply it to a wide variety of different food.

You gain more control over your environment when you use conceptual thinking. You avoid having to memorise details. Consequently you have more time for other activities and you increase your capacity to influence others if you can teach them concepts consistent with the way you think.

FOR EXAMPLE

You may decide to learn the recorder with your school-aged son or daughter. Maybe you start without a knowledge of music, but you can improve your understanding of a variety of musical concepts, without necessarily progressing to the clarinet or saxophone—unless you find you have hidden talent! This enables you to better communicate with your child, to be more influential in their lives, as well as improving your own capacity to appreciate music and increasing your *comfort* and *creativity* choices.

TIPS

- Remember that your brain is pre-programmed to learn and use concepts. It is the way your mind works naturally!
- Develop a concept-making attitude—be on the lookout for ways to put things together. Make notes, if this is helpful to you, and look for similarities and differences.
- Use the three Es—*exposure, experience* and *example*. It is obvious that you cannot learn to canoe from the river bank. Learning concepts often means you need to be immersed in the experience. To learn the theory of canoeing is fine, but you will learn so much more and develop the concepts better by exposure to the actual experience.

This is not only true for skills but also for tasks which are often thought of as cerebral. Learning foreign language concepts can best come, for example, from direct exposure to and experience with speakers of the foreign language in the culture and country where the language is spoken. To learn astronomy you need experience with telescopes, and to fully appreciate artistic or musical concepts you really need to have a go with a paintbrush or a musical instrument. It is not always necessary to perform at a high level to increase your conceptual understanding, enjoyment and development.

Growth through tools for off-loading learning

Happy people are not frantically busy all the time. They have enough space in their lives and their minds to focus some of their energy on growing. Furthermore, to keep adding to your learning you need an uncluttered mind. A major way in which you can create space in your life is by off-loading what you know and accessing it when you need it using notes and books.

In the past, there were certain advantages in making marks, to show territory, to record events, to help remember something that had been noticed. From these first steps writing developed. This skill is not something in your genetic inheritance. You are not born being able to read and write!

Nowadays there is voluminous knowledge available to us, but there is no need to carry around with you large chunks of information. You can use a range of tools, instruments and devices to put developments in thinking into storage. One of these is writing. There are other techniques. The way you do sums for example. Almost everybody uses calculators these days, and all you really need to know is the meaning of the process—you do not actually have to know all the steps in doing long division, but you do have to know what long division means to effectively use a calculator to do a long division sum.

Happy people are not frantically busy all the time. They have enough space in their lives and their minds to focus some of their energy on growing. To keep adding to your learning you need an uncluttered mind.

Drawings, diagrams and signs

Records themselves can become an aid for further thinking. When you record something by drawing, like the simple pulley on page 126, you are able to place the image of it in your mind and use your imagination to think of further ways it might be used. If you tried to put this into words it would go something like this: 'There is a wheel with grooves in it suspended from the ceiling; in the grooves there is a rope which can be turned,' and so on. Similarly, the image of, say, a pruning saw may help you see in your mind ways of reshaping a particular tree. So while written words are an important way of recording and an important thinking tool, so too are pictures, diagrams, numbers, charts, maps and graphs.

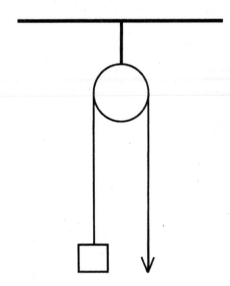

Drawings and diagrams help you make records and give you images that enhance your living. A simple sketch of the route to a particular spot gives you a better mind tool than a folder full of written instructions. From a happiness perspective it is worth remembering that diagrams and drawings are adaptable memory tools.

Sometimes you can transform a new work task into a drawing or a diagram. Not only will the effort of doing this help you to understand the new knowledge but it will also give you an aid to remembering the new task or process. In some training workshops, for example, participants are asked to describe a problem e.g. changes in their workplace management arrangements, by working together in small groups to produce a drawing to represent this change—often with startling results and new learning. (I've seen pictures of aeroplanes doing leaflet-drops as an example of management communication, and drawings of small boats being rowed to shore with sharks and giant squids representing various organisational dangers, swimming in the water beside them.)

Exercise 15: Drawing for growth

1. Draw a picture on a large sheet of paper using lots of colour. It could depict new arrangements introduced in your workplace; or how your local sporting club or church parish is run; or how the different members of the family are relating to the new child or new grandchild.

2. Share the picture you have drawn with a trusted friend or family member. Explain what you have drawn. Not only can this provide you with a record of your ideas on the topic, but also it will help you understand the situation.

3. Draw how you want it to look like in the future.

4. What can you do to help this visionary picture come about? Record your answers. Start implementing them!

Because drawings, diagrams and cartoons increase your understanding of the world and assist your memory, they offer the possibility of improving your happiness strike rate.

Signs and markers also act as records to remind you of things you need to do. You can order your life with these special indicators which your mind uses as a trigger.

FOR EXAMPLE

When older people move to a new environment they sometimes find that they cannot cope. It is usually not because they have somehow rapidly deteriorated (though the shock of change could produce this), or that their capacity for new learning may not be high, but rather that they have 'literally been separated from large parts of their minds[4]' which existed in the information stored in their homes—in the layout of their house; in the reminders of the sequence of activities to get breakfast; in the clocks, the television, the placement and type of heaters; in countless external aids to thinking.

The heart of using thinking tools is understanding their functions, not necessarily knowing all the processes. As complex tools like computers become increasingly user-friendly, you can maximise their capacity to assist you in your pursuit of happiness goals. To do this you need to understand clearly what they can do for you, not necessarily how the technology works—few of us know how to design computer programs—as you don't need to, unless that is your field of work.

Reading and writing

Writing is a tool to off-load information which we don't then have to store in our minds. Reading is the means by which we gain access to information off-loaded, either by ourselves or someone else. Reading is a source of recreation, ideas, gossip and teaching. It pervades every corner of your life. Everywhere you go there is something to read: the shop floor in a factory, a driving licence, a daily newspaper, the Internet, a bottle of beer, and on the television screen. People who are restricted in their reading skills are often considered handicapped. Nevertheless it is only since the last century that the majority of people have been taught to read and write. One effect of this has been to increase the knowledge and power of populations of whole countries.

It is what you choose to read and not to read that adds to, or detracts from, the further achievement of your happiness targets. Selectivity is the key to the successful use of reading material. Spending all your time reading is just as likely to limit the number of happiness goals you can achieve as spending all your time in front of a television set. You need to decide why you are reading and what you should read. What is it doing for you?

The purpose of reading to obtain a qualification you want is obvious enough. Recreational reading similarly needs to be adding to your *comfort*, *control*, or *creativity* if it is going to add to your happiness. Many forms of recreational reading will do this: by providing escape it can be a form of stress reduction, by giving you information on managing your money it can help you to control your income in your own interests and, by providing you with access to ideas, exposing your mind to new possibilities and by showing you ways to improve your productivity, it can enhance your development. The down side of recreational reading is when the time it uses in your life is excessive, or when the ideas themselves are counterproductive to your goals.

Film and television
Film and television are vehicles which you can use to help you reach more of your happiness goals. Essentially they have the capacity to provide the same kind of assistance as reading offers in a form well suited to the way your mind learns. They increase your thinking capacity, your ability to understand problems, issues, changes and fashions—they assist you to make improved choices in your lifestyle as you learn to laugh, sing, experience visual pleasure, excitement, and improve your health.

There is just one thing that you must be aware of when you use the visual media as a mind tool. As you have done with deciding what and when to read, you need to be selective. You need to ensure consistency of these tools with your own goals. Select a film or programme to watch, and measure it against your already-determined happiness goals.

Computers
Providing you have the right equipment, computers can deliver a large portion of the history and knowledge of our species. They provide a comprehensive extension to your mind. The term 'off-loading', which has been used in this chapter, owes it origin to computer jargon.

Computers share many of the same advantages and disadvantages as your other mind extension tools. Their huge capacity to access enormous amounts of information through the Internet is both a strength and a weakness.

Computers share many of the same advantages and disadvantages as your other mind extension tools. Their huge capacity to access enormous amounts of information through the Internet is both a strength and a weakness.

As well as learning about and seeing photographs of Mars, through NASA web sites, there is information on paedophilia and how to make a bomb.

Your computer usage is determined by what computer-accessed knowledge you interact with and how much time you spend doing it. As with the other extension tools of your mind, a key method of using a computer for happiness purposes is to match your use of it against your goals and not to become distracted along less productive paths.

There is no doubt that the computer is powerful tool. For a price, you can purchase all the current volumes of *Encyclopedia Britannica* on disk, ready for use on your computer. You can set up your own web page to introduce yourself to other Internet users across the world; you can arrange a date; send a letter; or book a room in a hotel almost anywhere in the world.

The potential for this mind extension tool to assist in the achievement of your happiness goals is substantial. This capacity, and any problems that computers may have, will increase as they become even more user-friendly, with, for example, programs being accessed by voice instructions, rather than by time-consuming keyboard inputs. In many ways, we are becoming more intelligent through these tools. Even current non-users may have available other family members who can do computer jobs for them.

Problems arise when computers are used to excess, and from using them in ways that do not enhance, or, more significantly, lead you away from your happiness goals.

Avoiding excessive use of computer games or other applications is achievable. It is like any other addiction or over-indulged activity—it can be overcome!

There are certain computer applications and technologically designed instruments with high potential for user excess. The most obvious of these are computer games. Avoiding excessive use of computer games or other applications is achievable. It is like any other addiction or over-indulged activity—it can be overcome!

These disadvantages are probably not experienced by most computer users. In any case, computers have become part of our world and will be used by increasingly larger numbers of people. If you the add to this the multiple television channel choice that cable/digital television brings, you have at your fingertips massive access to stored human knowledge and experience, which you can treat as an opportunity for growth.

This will happen, as long as you plan and focus your interactive hours so that you stay on your chosen path and still have enough time to do all the other things you need to do.

Clearly planning the time you spend on various parts of your life is extremely important. While you probably don't wish to be rigid, and I am not urging that, planning your non-paid activities is just as important to your happiness as planning your paid ones.

George's story: Growing into happiness

George's story is a long one, taking place over several years. This is a shortened version! George suffered an injury at work resulting in chronic pain especially to his back and shoulders. Despite several forms of surgery and continuous treatment, he still experiences pain. However, he also continues to work. He is the wage earner in his family of a wife and three children.

George's job is a repetitive one that includes manual assembly tasks, which he finds boring. As a younger man, his personal interests were physically active pursuits such as martial arts. Of course nowadays he is prevented from participating in these activities.

Over several years, his work and life restrictions (e.g. he is unable to lift and play with his young son, whom he dearly loves) led him to feel despondent and depressed, even to crying from time-to-time—something he hated doing. At times, he drank and smoked to relieve the emotional and physical pain. As well, he rested for long periods, which further decreased his involvement with his family.

With encouragement from others he started to build things by learning carpentry and welding skills from books. He was often quite pleased with his efforts and produced toys and small pieces of household furniture for his own and extended family. During the winter when his construction work was limited by his surroundings, as he worked mostly outside, he found he had little to do. With just a small amount of money he purchased a second-hand computer and began to teach himself how to use it and to learn keyboard skills.

For some time he had been reluctant to attend further education courses because he often felt he needed to move around, and, because of the pain, he found it difficult to concentrate for long periods. However, eventually he started a longer course, which included learning more information technology skills.

A major factor in the way George is coping with his difficulties is the growth in learning that he has made—growth that has improved his productivity, his feelings of self-worth, his contributions to his family, his personal enjoyment of life and his future.

Growth through improving your communication

Messages

A key part of growing and personal development is effective two-way communication. If a message is mixed or confused then obviously information or knowledge is rarely transmitted or received accurately.

FOR EXAMPLE

In my family there is a story about how my father, who lived in Adelaide, Australia, during World War II, came home from work and, in reference to the Japanese, announced to my mother: 'Well, they're here!' She, in great distress, thought 'they' were sailing up the local Port River, when in fact they had just bombed Darwin some two thousand kilometres away.

To achieve growth through communication, messages need to be given and received clearly. This includes constructive criticism. There is a training slogan, applicable to the area of personal growth and development, which says that 'feedback is the breakfast of champions'. If you can listen to and act on fair and reasonable and corrective advice, you will be able to improve your performance—a very desirable result!

TIPS

- To communicate in a meaningful and influential way with people you need to ensure that the way you are talking suits the person you are talking with—to do this you need to understand at least a little of their background. If you haven't this knowledge and if communication with them is important to you, you need to take the time to find out more about their communication style, and the meaning they give to the language they use. There are cultural differences in the way people learn to speak the same language and learn ideas through it. There are differences between people growing up in different cities in the same country, and even within the same city there are differences between different districts and different families. Some of these linguistic variations are well known—in America someone who is 'pissed' is angry, but in Britain it means you are inebriated. Sometimes because of life experiences, age, education or training there can be problems in communication even between members of the one family (as most of us know!).
- One way to try to learn a person's communication style is to visit the area that they come from: going to the shops, listening to the conversations, talking with other family members. People doing business in an entirely different culture can quickly become aware how important this background understanding is

for them, if they are to get their meaning across and conduct successful transactions (i.e. to exercise more control in terms of desired results). Even when two of us use the same words, it is no guarantee that we share the same meaning.

- You can check out, if you are unsure, the meaning of a conversation by asking clarifying questions such as, 'I am not sure what you mean by that. Could you explain that a bit more?' Unfortunately, you may have been taught not to ask questions. You may have learnt to think that if you ask a question you will make a fool of yourself by showing you do not understand. It is worth remembering that in group situations others may be keen to ask the same question as the one you want to ask. I've been surprised how often others ask the same question or make the same comment as the one that was on the tip of my tongue.

- Asking questions is a sign of intelligence. It is a demonstration of your desire to know. Asking questions does not have to be an attack on the speaker; it can often be seen by speakers as a sign of your interest. Questions can be put in a simple, non-threatening way such as, 'Could you help me understand that better?' 'I've had a late night, could you explain that to me again?' I am sure you don't want to get the speaker's stress levels up with questions which may be interpreted as confrontational.

- Your view is going to be accepted more readily if you are a credible person in the field you are talking about—a plumber does not necessarily have any better knowledge about the success of a sporting team than a dressmaker, butcher or the local doctor. In some instances, the opinion of a likely expert, say a psychologist, on how to raise children, might not be valued as highly as that of a local couple who are known to have successfully brought up several children. Politicians are often in this position: others often claim they know how to do the politician's job better than the politician. (I suspect there are many of us who feel this way!) If you want to have your views accepted then you need to be recognised as being knowledgeable either through recognised expertise or valued experience.

- Of course your opinions may be valued if what you are saying strikes a chord with the listener—if you are telling them what they want to hear. This is also a skill sought by politicians, but not one that is likely to enhance personal development, yours or anyone else's. To try to get people to like you by this often dishonest means is likely to cause you to feel dissatisfied with yourself. This kind of inner personal discontent will occur if your actions (words) do not match your thoughts. Your words may even backfire on you if the other person recognises their insincerity.

- The meaning you want to convey, if you are the speaker, is improved if it is backed up by your tone of voice, expression and body language—characteristics of the good storyteller. If you are reprimanding someone for a mistake it is not much use doing it with a big smile on your face—he or she won't think you are serious. Messages of undying love are not well received if they are given in an off-hand way while looking out the window. You need to look like you mean it as well as saying the words. Like acting, these are skills that can be enhanced with practice—even by doing them in front of a mirror.

- One easy way to develop your communication skills is to pay attention to the skills of those around you who give and receive messages well. Apply some of the techniques you see them using successfully.

Growth through creativity

Creativity

Creativity is not just a part of the lives of special people, artists, writers or dancers, rather it is a key aspect of all our lives. It is itself a happiness goal—most people would like to be more creative. It is also a means of increasing your satisfaction with your life.

When you are able to respond more creatively to a challenge, you are more likely to feel fulfilled (comfortable and in control). You can be creative in any part of your life. A creative

Creativeness has two phases. The first is the inspiration, the idea, the new insight phase, while the second is putting the idea into practice. In some instances, it is through engaging with a problem and struggling with it in different ways, that a person's creative capacity enables a new solution to be formed.

product is not just a new work of art—it can be a new recipe, a letter to a friend, or perhaps even new ways of managing cash flow. Nor is creativity restricted to producing something. It is also involved in how you respond in your relationships, your work, and in the kinds of attitudes you bring to living.

Creativeness has two phases. The first is the inspiration, the idea, the new insight phase, while the second is putting the idea into practice. In some instances it is through engaging with a problem and struggling with it in different ways, that a person's creative capacity enables a new solution to be formed. Even when this happens further work is usually required. Einstein is said to have 'dreamt up' his idea on relativity overnight and then he had to spend the next few years developing the mathematics to prove it.

Creativity is said to be governed by the right side of the brain. The left side governs the use of language and reasoning—it is this side that controls many of our conscious thoughts, while the right side helps us to be creative, often unconsciously.

Facets of creativity

There is little doubt that tapping your creative resources will enrich your life. Bear in mind that a well-cut diamond has many facets! Remember also that a particular strategy may serve different purposes. Practices, for example, which bring on the relaxation response also provide a good climate for the generation of creative responses.

You are unlikely to come up with good ideas when you are in a rage or very tense. Repeated experiences of relaxation may improve your general creative capacity. People who have worked regularly with hypnosis or meditation often report an expanded imaginative life. What you need from creative strategies is for them to improve your chances of reaching your happiness goals.

Creativity techniques

There are a number of ways of enhancing your creativity. A selection is provided below.

Open to sensory experiences
If you do not allow yourself to be open to sensory experiences you limit the free flow of potentially creative ideas. Sometimes you may not pay attention to the circumstances of your daily life: the colours, shapes, sights and smells. If you remain unaware of your surroundings you are not open to the possibilities that are offered by your creative right brain. The following small task illustrates this.

Exercise 16: Using your senses

- Write a description of an orange. Put that aside.
- Now take an actual orange—look at its shape and colour, smell its skin, feel it all over, notice what it feels like when you peel a piece, see what is on the inside skin and on the surface of the peeled orange, take a piece, notice if it squirts juice, put the piece in your mouth, feel it all over with your tongue, bite it, notice if you can hear anything, savour the taste.
- Now write another description of an orange.

Open to ideas
You, like the rest of us, probably have an inner censor in your mind that tells you to avoid certain ways of thinking, or that an action or idea is just wrong, stupid or illogical.

When you bring your inner critic into play you may close off creative possibilities. Brainstorming is a common method that works with a group to encourage a range of new ideas.

Using this technique all ideas suggested on a topic are taken on board; none are initially criticised—every comment is accepted.

You can do the same thing. Make a list, without initial evaluation, of anything that comes into your mind as a way of approaching a particular problem. Later you can assess in a logical, reasoning manner the particular merits of different solutions and ways of implementing them. Brainstorming brings into play both sides of our brain: perhaps the most important aspect of creativity addressed here is the need to be open in your thinking and not to rush to solutions until you have considered a number of options.

Forced reframes

Writers sometimes do this when they are writing about a situation, and they choose another situation as a way of redescribing the original circumstances. A writer might, for example, be describing the inside of a house and choose something unrelated that is then used to describe the house. Let us say they choose the sea as their unrelated context. The description might then go like this: 'Each room flowed into the next. There didn't seem to be any boundaries. The odd scarf and tie was draped over sofas and chairs like so much discarded seaweed left stranded from the outgoing tide of activity the previous night.' This approach can be applied to other kinds of problems. You might, for example, have an office problem that you could describe in terms of a farm, a shopping centre, a tree, or a swimming complex.

Forced reframes can be applied to recreational and home problems, as well as work situations.

By seeing your problem in a different way, you open up other possible solutions—ones you may not have thought of if you had stuck to a traditional, logical, step-by-step approach. Reframing is a technique that can be applied to recreational and home problems, as well as work situations.

'Wrong' handwriting

Wrong-handed writing is a way of releasing understanding from our right brain.[5] This approach involves using the hand you don't write with for writing the answers to questions you may have. Or you could make a list of what you need to do to solve a problem, and then list the most important features of the problem.

While you may find it awkward to write in this way, persevere: you may find the results surprising. This will be because the responses will be less likely to be coming from a critical perspective and more likely to be focused on creative, new or inventive messages.

Wrong-handed writing is a way of releasing understanding from our right brain. You may find the results surprising!

Creativity products

Experiencing someone else's creativity can be a part of the magic of living.

FOR EXAMPLE

When I was a young child I stayed overnight at Uncle Charlie's place. We had rabbit for tea. After the meal Uncle Charlie put the rabbit bones that remained in a saucepan and covered them with water. He hinted to me that something miraculous would happen overnight.

The next morning the bones had gone and the saucepan was full of reddish 'rabbit jam', which had the flavour of strawberries. While I now know the truth of the matter, Uncle Charlie's magic has remained with me all my life and still gives me pleasure.

Music in all its variations—the young still keep inventing new forms—brings sweet pleasure to its creators and its listeners. You can also select from plays, books, films, opera and dance for your inspiration, recreation, joy and new learning.

Contemporary films, for example, can be a source of new ideas, suggesting different approaches to life. Additionally, you can nurture your friendships through the discussion of shared meanings that help you to make sense of the world.

Creative products as well as creative processes are a valuable source of personal growth.

Creative products as well as creative processes are a valuable source of personal growth. Another way of growing is in relationships with others, which is taken up in the next section.

Summary

You have learnt how growth, as a means to happiness, can come from:

- learning concepts and using them for your benefit.
- using off-loading and mind extension tools. (The tools reviewed included writing and reading, film, television and computers.)
- learning to use communication as a form of growth.
- learning about creativity, practising creativity techniques, such as openness to sensory experiences, forced reframes and wrong handwriting and enjoying the products of creativity.

PRINCIPLE 5
OTHERS MATTER

Other people and you

Closeness and intimacy

When you relate well to another person you might sometimes say that you can 'put yourself in their shoes'—you recognise what they feel when they have been hurt or when they laugh— you can see a situation through their eyes. You could say you have empathy for them.

It has been suggested that as you closely associate with other people you may even interact mentally. One author[6] writing about shared mental processing, describes different situations where you may experience another's feelings: a leader may experience his or her followers' aspirations and feelings; a mother may feel her baby as an extension of herself; and, with very close friends or partners, in physical and non-physical intimacy, you can get 'inside' each other. At the extreme you may assume some of the other person's behavioural character- istics. Things like sharing the same expressions, using the other person's special sayings or mannerisms, or finishing your part- ner's sentence are fairly common occurrences.

Intimacy, nevertheless, is *not* about becoming confused and losing your identity, but rather about knowing and understanding the other person intimately. We have already established that the separateness of knowing yourself and recognising your personal worth are important. So though intimacy is equally important, it shouldn't be allowed to infringe on your sense of self.

You can become different as a consequence of this process of intimacy. In one sense it can be a value-added extra to the kind of learning you get from your personal teachers—family, friends, peers, the media, and so on. Intimacy is an opportunity to share other people's ideas and their experiences. In terms of your happiness, it is better for you if their experiences are good ones.

Intimacy is an opportunity to share other people's ideas and their experiences.

Even from a self-centred view you need to take account of the concerns and happiness of others as their wellbeing affects you. Just living life for yourself may not produce the results you expect.

Problems with other people

The French playwright, Jean Paul Sartre, once wrote a play where, in the after-life, people of quite different attitudes, values and personalities were forced to live together. This was truly hell.

Quentin Crisp, who was a well-known English public figure, was quoted as saying 'other people are a mistake'.

At some time in your life you have probably felt harmed, humiliated, saddened, angered or frustrated by another person. This happens even when you know that how you respond emotionally is often a matter of what you are doing in your head as much as what is actually being said or done.

These negative images of other people emphasise your separateness from others, competition with them and your own isolation. Happiness on the other hand lies in maximising the advantages that can come from your inevitable connectedness.

While you may need at times to be independent, you also need to know effective ways of relating and ways to overcome differences. All relationships take place in a context—as a couple, a family, in a group or at work. While the central focus in this section is on personal relationships, many strategies (e.g. managing disagreement) can be applied in more than one context.

Allan's story: Finding a personal connection

Allan was in his mid-fifties. He had a long history of unemployment, periods in prison, and spasmodic alcoholic binges. At the time the relevant part of his story begins, he had just joined a men's group, where he was surprised to find others who had similar life experiences.

After he had revealed his background to the group, Fred, another group member, said that he thought he knew Allan's daughter, with whom Allan had had no connection for many years. Allan agreed that Fred should approach his (Allan's) daughter to see if they might reconnect.

Fred reported back that his daughter thought him pretty much an old reprobate and didn't want anything to do with him. However, he also added that his daughter had a child, a little girl, who was now nine or ten years old. Allan thought this was 'pretty good'. He was pleased to see himself as a grandparent.

The faithful Fred made yet another visit to the daughter, who agreed that if her daughter wanted to she could see her grandfather and, for whatever reason, the grand-daughter agreed to this—perhaps she was just curious.

As the daughter still didn't wish to see her father, Fred acted as the go-between and arranged a meeting on neutral territory between the two relatives—granddaughter and grandfather.

They have continued to meet ever since, and, with the separation of a generation, get on well with each other. Since that time Allan has had a different view of life—he can see positive events in his future; he has someone of his own to whom he can relate. Allan has become involved in voluntary work and has been attending literacy classes.

Couples, marriage and other relationships

'Relationship' in the present context is a contemporary expression, dating from the mid-twentieth century. It is used to refer to any kind of coupling of some arbitrary duration longer than a fleeting encounter. While relationships, including marriages, may not be expected to be permanent, they are commonly expected to be stable. As one leading figure in the entertainment industry put it: 'I only have one relationship at a time!' This could be called serial monogamy. In this context, instability is seen as having two or three relationships concurrently, or perhaps a succession of fleeting ones.

Mixed messages are given on how to behave in a family or a partnership, with guilt being the pay-off for those who think they have got it wrong. Of course, there are a plethora of agony aunt columns, magazine articles, and family forums offering you advice, but let's start with some facts.

Couple facts

- In 2001, the marital status of the British population over fifteen years old was:

    40.5 per cent married (includes a number of re-marriages, that is former divorcees)

    2.0 per cent separated (still legally married)

    44.3 per cent never married (includes other forms of relationships)

    6.4 per cent were divorced

    6.7 per cent were widowed.

- In 1998, 28.8 per cent of people who married were living together before marriage.

- There has been an increase in cohabitation in Great Britain. Among non-married women aged under 60, the proportion cohabiting more than doubled from 13 per cent in 1986 to 28 per cent in 2001. For men it also more than doubled over the same period from 12 per cent to 25 per cent. Higher proportions of divorced people in Great

Britain cohabit compared with other marital statuses: 34 per cent of divorced men and 30 per cent of divorced women lived in a cohabiting relationship in 2001.

• Since 1971, the number of marriages in the United Kingdom has fallen from around 459,000 to just over 286,000 in 2001. The number of divorces increased from just under 80,000 in 1971 and peaked in 1993 at 180,000. The number of divorces then fell by 13 per cent to 157,000 in 2001.[7]

None of these statistics actually tell us the percentage of the total population who could be described as being 'in a relationship' at any one period in time. If you take into account gay relationships and non-statistically declared *de facto* couples as well as marriages and other recognised relationships, then the percentage of people in a relationship is likely to be more than 70 per cent of adults. Most of us are, have been, or will be in a relationship. And, if you aren't, it seems you often think you ought to be.

Perhaps relationship issues sometimes need to be taken less seriously.

FOR EXAMPLE
A piece of grafitti I once saw scribbled on a wall read: 'My mother made me a homosexual.' Written underneath in different handwriting was: 'If I buy her some wool will she make me one too?'

In our search for happiness, getting on with our partner is of considerable importance. To relate effectively as men and women means understanding our differences as well as resolving our disputes.

Women and men—power over others
The exercise of the control in relationships is an enduring issue, particularly men's control of women. During the last hundred years or so many women have reacted to this

situation—from the political action of suffragettes fighting for the vote, to concern about the glass ceiling in the business world today keeping women out of boardrooms and top managerial positions. The media has itself reacted to its own past advocacy and has in recent years very much promoted a changing role of increasing public responsibility and occupational opportunity for women. This particular pendulum is swinging again. Many social commentators are saying: 'What about men?' and 'What about boys?' There is also some public criticism of the role of politically correct language as a social equaliser. Does using politically correct language promote change or simply mask inequalities? The messages are often confusing. Who is right? Who is wrong? How could what was 'right' last year be 'wrong' this year? It doesn't make planning for happiness easy whether you are a man or a woman.

In the final analysis, power over someone is often as much structural as verbal. I have known male business, institutional and group leaders who have adopted politically correct gender language, but who have also found ways of curtailing female power within the group or organisation.

Power over someone is often as much structural as verbal. I have known male business leaders who have adopted politically correct gender language, but who have also found ways of curtailing female power within their group or organisation.

Women's business, men's business

Much is made of the differences in attitudes and behaviour of women and men. The issue here is understanding differences and then using this understanding to act in ways that complement the happiness goals of your partner.

While not everyone agrees on the kinds of differences that exist between women and men, it is obvious that there are biological distinctions. Doubt arises over whether behaviour, such as physical aggression on the part of men and nurturing on the part of women, are natural, that is are they part of your 'hard wiring', or have you learnt them since birth from your teachers? Perhaps it is a combination of the two. The argument about whether our genes or our environment influences us most is far from settled.

In daily life there are differences, which is not to say they should be encouraged or discouraged but just that they are there. It may be possible to take the 'girl' out of Barbie to create Feral Cheryl but it is certainly more difficult to find real living girls without at least some Barbie attitudes. Just as many girls seem to end up playing with dolls and acting out nurturing roles, many boys seem to participate in controlling and aggressive games. While promotion, advertising and culture have a large part to play in this, it seems unlikely that they are the sole cause.

The differences between the way men and women can behave needs to be taken into account in relationships. The obvious physical differences between the sexes are indisputable. Less obvious are some biological differences such as hormonal distinctions that nonetheless can affect feelings and consequent behaviour. Then, of course, there are the gender differences in social behaviour, which often exist irrespective of whether their origin is organic or learnt. These differences are shown in wide-ranging activities, such as nurturing styles (e.g. men tend to be protective and women supportive) or household chores (e.g. men tend to do outside jobs and women inside ones). Even when role changes are adopted the different behaviour, however, can have a residue of earlier attitudes: 'He expects to be knighted when he does the washing up.' 'So she put the rubbish out—*big deal!*'

Just by taking account of nurturing activities, recognising them and responding to them, a male partner can become himself more nurturing. By listening and sharing in the strategies described in 'Tips on getting agreement' (page 150) both partners will be acting in a more constructive way.

Recognising and accepting differences is also obviously important. Retired couples, for example, may need to allow for the opportunity for separate activities. Men and women, living at home together both need their domains of work, or as one researcher suggests, their separate 'sheds'.[8]

Even with clear understanding disagreements are to be expected in every relationship.

Fight until you drop

In the film *The War of the Roses*, the couple engage in continuous skirmishing until they die fighting.

FOR EXAMPLE

A couple I knew of fought frequently. They went to a lawyer to see about arranging for a divorce. After waiting for some time, they got up and left, telling the receptionist that if they couldn't be attended to they wouldn't bother going on with it!

Some couples seem to enjoy the battlefield of domestic dispute; others prefer a more harmonious and pleasant environment.

How to disagree

Perhaps the first step towards harmonious decision-making is knowing how to disagree. The three most common approaches to disagreement are *aggression*, *compliance* and *assertion*.

Aggression is when you respond to a situation by demanding that your 'rights' prevail. Let's look at an example. You are discussing going on a visit. You say: *Why you want to visit your Aunt Maude amazes me. You know how she annoys me. We are just not going there.*

Compliance is when you accept the situation without commenting, but feel frustrated and upset underneath by your partner's lack of consideration. In this instance, you say nothing and go on the visit to Aunt Maude, feeling upset.

Assertion is when you let your feelings be known without demanding your 'rights'. You may say: *I often feel upset going to visit Aunt Maude. Is there something else we could do?* Thus you leave the way open for other possibilities, including going to visit Aunt Maude if that seems the most suitable option and one that you can agree to 'grin and bear'.

Aggression is a demand for control, which is hardly the basis for a good partnership. Compliance hides your true feelings and you risk building up resentment against your partner. Again, this is not a good recipe for the future. It is only when you use assertion that you are disclosing all, but at the same time showing your consideration.

Counsellors often call assertive comments 'I' statements. They are an honest and practical way of making your views known. When you make them you are not saying anything about the other person, you are only saying something about yourself.

Exercise 17: Making 'I' statements

1. To learn to make 'I' statements, if you do not already use them, requires practice. First list four situations where you would disagree, or would want to disagree with your partner.
2. Write down what you would say or would think but not say. Change these words or thoughts into statements like, 'I feel upset when such and such happens,' or 'When I am trying to . . . I feel . . . ' or 'When I notice . . . I feel . . . .'

It is important to not trick yourself into going down the aggressive path by saying something like, 'I feel upset when you do . . . .' Although you have begun the statement with 'I feel' you are bringing in criticism of the other person. Assertion is about expressing your feelings and your needs. To use these statements, which you have worked out in advance of an actual incident, requires rehearsal and practice.

Although 'I' statements can lead to less conflict, it is not a way of stopping all fights. It can, however, diminish their intensity and improve the quality of the argument, helping you both to achieve a better result.

TIPS

The tips on communication and creativity techniques (pages 133–39), such as being open to ideas, can be combined with other strategies to provide steps that are usually helpful in reaching a decision suitable to both of you.

1. Listen carefully and without interruption to each other. This is often not as easy it sounds, as your thoughts may run ahead to what you want to say, and when this happens you are likely to stop listening to the other person.
2. One way of knowing you have been listening carefully is to think whether you can put in your own words what the other person has said and have them agree that this was what they meant.
3. If you cannot easily summarise what the other person has been saying, it is okay to ask clarifying questions (e.g. 'Can you tell me more?' 'Could you explain what you mean?').
4. Try to avoid leaping to answers or solutions straight away.
5. Look for information about the problem that might be helpful.
6. Brainstorm ideas (put down all your ideas without arguing about them). This ensures that you do not neglect possible answers.
7. Work through the possibilities together.

This approach to getting agreement is better suited to, say, deciding on a holiday or other project, than working out who sweeps the kitchen floor. However, even in the latter example, it might be sensible to go through an agreement exercise to look at sharing a number of simple household tasks, rather than considering them one at a time. If you disagree about who should do them, a joint decision may be needed; in which case the seven-step approach above would be worthwhile.

Attachment and freedom

Issues involving attachment and freedom are relevant to achieving happiness in families and at work, as well as in the narrower couple context.

Perhaps two of the most substantial fears you can experience are the fear of being alone and alternatively the fear of having to be with someone or a group.

In the first instance, the fear is about listening to your inner voice which may be doubting and self-critical; it is about being unsure; it is about having to face the issues of life alone, unaided and frightened. When you are like this, other people may describe you as vulnerable. If you feel like this, you could be falling out of one relationship and rebounding into another. To constantly seek a relationship no matter what, to be desperate for one, to value attachment above all else, is what this fear engenders. Clearly these are not ways of acting that will enhance your *comfort* and *control*. On the contrary, they are pursuits in which you are likely to surrender your self-control to others and perhaps put up with considerable discomfort because the alternative of being alone is even more frightening. People who have broken the merry-go-round of relationship-chasing are those who have learnt to be more self-assured and more confident about being able to manage life's stresses and strains. Such learning can occur through discussions with supportive friends and through self-development including practising some of the self-confidence building exercises suggested in this book (pages 50, 116–17).

Fortunately few people are caught in a long succession of unhappy relationships. Nevertheless, it is easily apparent that your happiness in a relationship can be improved if you are self-assured and can comfortably spend time alone. Being a couple does not mean you must be constantly interacting. There should be time for peace and solitude.

People who have broken the merry-go-round of relationship-chasing are those who have learnt to be more self-assured.

Time to be alone to walk around the garden, watch your special television programme, exercise, listen to music, or to meditate or pray. These periods of reflection and separateness give you further strength to be accepting, loving and to develop your relationship further when you *are* with your partner. It is helpful therefore to you, as well as to your partner, if you make it easy for there to be times of *re-creation*.

Vulnerability is also a feature of being frightened to be with someone. When you feel this way you are afraid that by letting someone get close to you they will see your weaknesses and imperfections and, as well, that you may lose control of parts of your life. Desire for freedom rather than attachment may spring from healthy self-confidence but, in this context, it is based on concerns and worries, and can include a fear of rejection. When this fear is felt to a strong degree it can lead to constantly avoiding entanglement with others for fear of exposing your shortcomings and being subsequently hurt. Overcoming such difficulties is possible using the same self-confidence building strategies as those proposed above to overcome the fear of being alone. It also involves having a go even if you are afraid. The more you expose yourself to a fear the easier it becomes to face it again. From increased trust in your own capacity to cope with criticism comes an increased willingness to risk being criticised and so to risk forming a relationship.

For most of us in a relationship the message is again clear: improve your self-confidence and you will be able to share more of yourself (strengths and weaknesses) and so improve the quality of your interactions and the happiness that stems from them.

Neither attachment (dependence) nor freedom (independence) are happiness goals in themselves. What matters in a relationship is that you maintain the capacity to support a partner and share life's activities with them, as well as being able to act alone.

An effective and loving relationship is interdependent.

Compatibility

Over the last fifty years much has been said and written about compatibility. Many institutions run pre-marriage courses and of course popular magazines are full of questionnaires and articles on how to find a suitable partner.

While learning how to disagree reasonably may be helpful, sometimes couples may have differences that are difficult to reconcile. Family therapists will tell you that disputes most commonly occur over money, relatives, sex and children.

Compatibility in part relates to sharing similar views, not necessarily over what should be done, but often over how it should be done—it is not whether you should use toothpaste or not, but rather what end of the tube you should squeeze. When issues about money arise, couples often share similar financial objectives but they may have different ideas on how they should be achieved. What is to be given priority—a new stove or fridge, or an electric drill, or a weekend away? How is a decision to be made? Together, by the one who earns the most, by the partner whose turn it is, by the one who threatens the most? What methods of obtaining financial resources are to be used—by saving, borrowing from friends or relatives or a finance company, lay-by, selling something, gambling, or by hoping something will turn up? It is not difficult to see how different approaches by partners can conflict.

The problem with measuring the compatibility of two people is that there are exceptions to most of the common wisdom on this topic. You probably know of happy couples very different in personality, but who get on well, or couples who come from different walks of life or who have very different occupations, yet seem to share a happy life together. Professionals can also find understanding relationships complex! One book written for therapists has the title *One Couple: Four Realities* and deals with the four different ways the same couple could be treated by four different styles of therapy.[9] So a normal relationship is complex and multi-layered. There will always be a variety of viewpoints to be aired but this also usually means that a couple will be able to come up with a variety of solutions to a problem.

You probably know of happy couples, very different in personality, but who get on well. To get on together you need to have some matching values and some agreement about the way you should do things. To know what is important to you both and what you can understand about each other will help you to achieve your happiness goals. The exercise below is designed to do that.

Exercise 18: Exploring what matters in your relationship

You may need to spread this exercise over at least two occasions. It has two parts—one is comparing your happiness goals and the other is comparing how you do things. Again the exercise is meant to be enjoyable and not a chore, or source of argument.

Happiness goals

1. If your partner has not done Exercise 2, page 40, have him or her complete it (assuming they agree to participate).
2. Compare your results. To what extent do you agree? Are there areas in which you can agree to differ? Are there areas in your lives where you might need to make some changes? What might they be? Note them.

Ways of doing things

To do this part of the exercise you are asked to separately and independently write down points on each of four aspects of your relationship.

1. Describe how you would like your money managed. This may be the same as at present or it may be different. You should include who pays what and how (e.g. cash, cheque or credit card).

_____

_____

_____

2. Describe the three aspects of relating sexually that you believe are important. This may include times and timing, place or clothing as well as sexual behaviour itself.

_____

_____

_____

3. Describe the kinds of arrangements you would like to have with both sets of relatives. This includes who you would or wouldn't prefer to visit, how often you want them to visit, when (night or day, weekend or during the week) and what their visits to you would be like (e.g. to stay overnight, a week or for a meal).

_____

_____

_____

4. List three aspects of bringing up children that you think are important. Be specific. If, for example, you say discipline, describe how you would do this. Even if you don't have children you could still answer this last point. It may offer some useful insights.

_____

_____

_____

5. After you have completed your separate sets of descriptions you can compare your answers and see where you agree and where you may need to adjust or compromise. It is important that you don't expect

a perfect match. What your partner values and their actions do not have to coincide perfectly with your views and actions. Acceptance of differences is a constructive attitude. Knowing how you are different can help you work out strategies to avoid conflict. If there are difficulties, remember you can use 'Tips on getting agreement' (page 150).

Maria's and Lou's story: Improving compatibility

Maria and Lou had been married for more than ten years. They waited a while before having children. At the time this story commences, they had three children. From their own view of their marriage, and from the opinion of their friends as well, it was considered that they had a contemporary marriage with a good understanding of gender issues. They were both tertiary educated and working in human resources.

When they entered counselling, Maria complained that they were not 'getting on' and that Lou was not pulling his weight. For his part, Lou claimed that he was but that Maria was not noticing what he did and how he contributed to the marriage. Maria said that she wanted to be more of a partner in the relationship with the role of mother coming second.

The first task they were given as a couple was to notice what each other did and to list the different family jobs they performed. They were then asked what they noticed about the list (and other analysing questions). They found in their own words that the jobs fell into night-time and day-time time jobs and outside and inside ones. It came as a surprise to them to find that these jobs were sorted mainly along gender lines (i.e. Lou did most outside jobs), since they believed that they had the household roles balanced.

Their next steps were to swap some of their jobs and consider the experiences involved. Another task was to set aside 'couple time'. Once a fortnight one of them would take sole responsibility for providing the couple time. This would include arranging for a baby-sitter, buying the tickets to the pictures, booking the table at a restaurant, or ensuring that the car had petrol in it to take them to the beach where they could go for a walk—the outing did not need to be expensive. They thought this was a good idea but initially found it hard to do. Eventually they had a weekend away to celebrate their wedding anniversary.

An important factor in their success was that they were both committed to doing things differently to change how they felt.

Maria's and Lou's experiences give an example of how to develop an understanding of each other and improve compatibility. Similarly they emphasise the need to pause and notice what is happening rather the jumping to conclusions (one of the steps in reaching agreement). Finally, exploring their jobs by interchanging them, draws to their attention their own necessary interdependence.

Getting the message

A key factor in your happiness, not just in your relationship with your partner, but also in most social and work activities, is the extent to which the messages of others are actually understood. Their meaning is important.

FOR EXAMPLE

I heard perhaps the best praise I've have ever had when our family were living in England and one of my children described me to his teacher as an Australian mind reader! While this was unfortunately neither true nor justified my joy at receiving such an accolade was because the child understood about meaning and thought I did too.

Meaning is based on 'reading between the lines' of the conversation, recognising the body language and learning from experience. If you can recognise and correctly interpret another's message, then you can 'read their minds'. If your partner says, for example, 'Nothing is the matter,' in response to a question from you, it may simply mean that they want some time to think about it. There is no need to interpret it as a rejection of you. What people do and say is generally about them. Thus when a person cries or gets angry they are expressing how they feel. Even your partner's criticism of you stems from their feelings and needs, and how they are seeing things, even though it may have been something you said or did that provided the trigger.

The closer you are to someone, the more you are likely to experience that intimacy of minds described earlier. Which of these sayings is true? 'Absence makes the heart grow fonder' or 'Out of sight, out of mind'? When there is a strong union of spirit, aspirations and hope, a relationship is best able to handle separation. Separations for extended periods, such as working or studying elsewhere, can break up some relationships, while others endure and become stronger on reunion. The more you are concerned about the welfare and happiness of the other person (above your own), the more likely intimacy will be enhanced and the more likely your own wellbeing will be improved. There is joy in caring.

Friends and community

Friends, groups and community

The need for mutually supportive contact with other people in developing your sense of happiness is the recurring theme in this section. It is a view in conflict with those commercial and social messages telling you that your sole focus should be yourself—the so-called 'me generation' perspective. Having good friends is not only an important contributor to your daily living, but is also a valuable source of support when you are troubled. To have friends it is also necessary to be one.

At times, you may feel you are too busy with your job, partner or family to follow your interests in an organised way by joining one of the many sporting, recreational, educational, religious or self-help groups in your neighbourhood. If you do have other interests, other places to go, especially if they have a social aspect to them, you are less likely to feel stranded in times of personal transition, such as retirement, divorce or loss of a loved one.

As the number of families with one or two children has increased there has been a parallel decrease in the extended family support of relatives. This change, coupled with a greater tendency to move to different neighbourhoods, towns or cities has reduced our sense of community.

The idea that you are living in a community can be a source of security (comfort). Irrespective of their effectiveness, schemes such as Neighbourhood Watch can foster this feeling of community. Community can also improve your feeling of control over your life by providing a place and an environment where you know where to go to get help with the plumbing, or the electricity, or to have your health needs met and where your children can go to scouts or dance classes. Therefore the message is: make every effort to be a helpful and considerate neighbour, to participate in local community exercises, such as jumble sales, school functions or sporting clubs, and to nurture on-going friendships.

People at work

Work sites are places of considerable person-to-person interaction. They provide opportunities for you to learn about yourself and achieve more of your happiness goals. Ideas we have considered already, such as how to reach agreement, how to be relaxed, calm and cool, or how to use creativity techniques are applicable to your working life. Here are some other important points.

TIPS

- *Focus on the task, not the position.*

  Work activities are enjoyed most when you are paying attention to them, rather than seeing how they can be used to get the next promotion, the next job, more money, or time off, or how you can avoid doing them tomorrow! This is not meant to suggest you should be a 'wage slave', but simply that absorption in tasks is likely to make you happier than trying to wish the present work away.

- *Remember that in a work context your greatest strength may be your greatest weakness.*

  Someone, for example, who is good at reaching compromises may at times need to be quite clear and direct with workmates or supervisors about what should or should not be done. While their skill at negotiation will often be helpful, there will be times when, for their own benefit as well as others, a less compromising approach will be necessary. Similarly, a strong authoritarian style will be helpful occasionally, but will need to be put aside at other times. If you are aware of your skills, you always need to check if they are applicable to a particular situation rather than just proceeding because 'that's the way you do things'.

- *Rarely do anything yourself that someone else can do as well or better.*

  While this principle is the kind of advice generally given to managers, it can be applied to situations where workers have different skills. This may include not only the skills that go with the description of their job, but others that the person brings to the job. Simple examples of this are where one person happens to be physically stronger than another or more nibble-fingered, or better with a computer or better at composing letters. Sharing skills is a satisfying as well as an effective way of going about your business.

- *Recognise that teamwork can be enjoyable.*
  Unfortunately, there are some situations where this may not be possible. If you are a lift operator there may not be much scope for teamwork. However, even if you cannot control how jobs are done in your work site, you may find opportunities to promote team approaches. Not only is this often more satisfying, but it also often provides a more productive and intelligent result.
- *Make a clear distinction between your work role and your home or recreational self.*
  You are not going to improve your work productivity or help yourself when you bring work home in your head. If there are times when work has to be done at home, clear boundaries need to be drawn, usually in terms of fixed times. Say to yourself, 'I'll stop work on this project every day at 5.30 p.m.,' or 'I'll work on that report between 8.00 a.m. and noon on Saturday.'

  Whether your work is at home, in the office or the factory, *transition times* can be helpful. When you are on your way home from work, pull over, stop the car for ten minutes and listen to some relaxing music, read the newspaper, or just watch the other cars go by. Transition activities can also include having a coffee with someone after work, going to the gym or a sporting activity, or going for a walk.

  Towards the end of such transition times you should spend a minute or two to remind yourself to focus on the new role you are going to undertake outside work, as a father or mother, or as someone's partner and listener, or as a cook, gardener, or any combination of these or similar roles.

Other people are a part of you. Your continued personal development can be improved by increasing the fruitfulness of your relationships at play and at work. You can have a hand in these changes even though you may not control all the players or 'call all the shots'.

Summary

You have learnt:

- how you are inevitably bound up with the aspirations and desires of others.
- that to be in a relationship is a common goal.
- how understanding differences between the sexes can help your relationship.
- what you can do to improve the quality of your disagreements as well as reaching better agreements.
- that being alone sometimes can be a strength rather than a weakness in a relationship, and that a successful relationship is one characterised by interdependence rather than complete independence or dependence.
- how you can explore compatibility.
- how important it is to understand another person's message.
- that relating to friends and participating in the community is highly desirable.
- strategies you can use to improve your happiness at work and its connection to the rest of your life.

PRINCIPLE 6
KNOWING IS RARELY
ENOUGH

There are likely to be times in your life when you know you need to change; give up an old habit, or start a new one. You may even know what you have to do (give up smoking, exercise more or put aside time for recreation) without always being sure how to do it. And even when you know how, it is sometimes difficult to find the motivation, the will or the desire to do it. Sometimes you may feel you have become dependent on that habit for your happiness.

There are other situations when knowing is rarely enough. You may feel upset because of a trauma experience or loss of a loved one. It is reasonable to be sad, but you may not know how to move on with your life or how to help a friend move on with theirs (remembering that your feelings are tied up with their experiences).

There are ways of managing the feelings associated with both these kinds of experiences that can improve your comfort and control—your happiness.

In this chapter, we look at how to change habits and how to live with unavoidable events.

Dependence on nicotine, alcohol or other drugs

To find relief from the problems and stresses of life by smoking, drinking alcohol, or ingesting prescription sedatives, anti-depressants, or illegal drugs is to run the risk of becoming dependent on them. Temporary happiness or numbness is rarely sustained and, even more unfortunately, it can cause new problems (e.g. health difficulties from smoking) or make your old problems seem worse when the effect of the drug has worn off.

If you are dependent on a substance you feel physiological discomfort (or even pain) when the substance is withdrawn. One of the most powerful drugs is nicotine. It is sometimes said that in a purely biological sense it is as powerful as some illegal drugs. Heroin and alcohol have multiple other effects. Using heroin produces, among other things, a greater state of euphoria or intoxication than nicotine—it takes you away from your present feelings entirely.

Drug dependency also involves psychological discomfort when the drug is withdrawn. If you have given up smoking you have probably experienced the difficulty in changing how you see yourself (no longer a 'smoker', now a 'non-smoker') and in trying to forget the memory of the tension-releasing feeling that you felt smoking gave you. Even though the symptoms of physiological withdrawal may be gone in perhaps even a few days, the memories of what smoking felt like and how you identified with it may stay for a long time. It is probably for this reason that people stop smoking then start again many times.

The good news is that the more you try the more likely you will finally succeed. This is true for changing most habits. It is important to remember that a failed attempt may be a step that can lead you to a successful one. Don't give up!

Psychological dependency may have other features if, for example, you have taken alcohol or drugs to escape from worries. When this happens, it seems better to be intoxicated than to face unpleasant difficulties (often associated with feelings of poor self-worth). In these circumstances, it is not only necessary to get rid of the physiological addiction, but also to gain control over your life and to improve how you feel about yourself and others. This usually means having in place outside support and self-help strategies.

One view of alcohol addiction says that if you abuse alcohol you need to accept yourself as a failure in controlling your drinking; seek the support of a higher power and the support of others with similar experiences; recognise your addiction by being able to say, for example, 'I am an alcoholic', and consider that it is failure to drink any alcohol. In part, this is the position of Alcoholics Anonymous (AA). Their approach has clearly been helpful for many people, and other self-help groups have adapted these methods.

There is another view which encourages less self-blaming if lapses occur. It is a view that sees a lapse as an opportunity to remind you what you need to do to avoid future lapses. Health professionals who support this strategy believe that when a single lapse is seen as a minor aberration which can be easily corrected you are more likely to get back quickly onto the rehabilitation programme. When a single lapse is seen as a failure, this is more likely to lead to feelings of devastation and a rapid fall back into old habits.

If success is measured in abstinence, then both approaches have their successes, and some people seem more suited to one than the other. Some people, for example, find it difficult to identify with the semi-spiritual nature of Alcoholics Anonymous or similar programmes, or the idea that total abstinence is required. On the other hand, the support of others is generally critical to the success of a rehabilitation programme, especially those who are in recovery: AA has this in abundance.

FOR EXAMPLE

Let us imagine I was on a diet and I went to a friend's place for a barbecue and all they had were sausages—I do love sausages!

I ate the sausages until I could eat no more. There are at least two ways I can react to this. I could say to myself: 'You are a pig, a self-indulgent glutton, who is headed for obesity. You are a failure. You might as well eat sausages everyday for breakfast,' or I could say: 'You enjoyed those sausages, but that doesn't mean you have to keep eating them. Let this day be a signal to remind you to eat other food.'

For those seeking to manage habits of excess or many of life's other difficulties, there will be 'sausage days'. The key to happiness is not whether there are down times, but how we handle them when they occur.

Dependence on gambling, work or sex

As well as through substance abuse it is possible to lose happiness by becoming too involved in activities that are often considered part of our everyday living and even, at particular times, a source of happiness.

Gambling, for example, can become an all-consuming part of your life. You may become addicted to poker machines because you know that a payout can occur, but never know when this will happen. When a reward of variable size comes irregularly and unpredictably, it is a powerful form of training. Because you don't know when the goodies are going to come you may keep playing. Alternatively, or additionally, you may find gambling becomes a source of emotional thrills and absorption, taking you away from your problems. In this kind of situation gambling is a release that can be compared in some ways to alcohol. For a percentage (some say as low as four per cent, others say a higher figure) of people who gamble, gambling becomes a major continuing, and sometimes destructive, part of their life.

Sex or work can also be used as an escape from life's troubles. Sexual activities or sexual aberrations can become an addictive source of pleasure—which in extreme cases becomes a destructive force when sexual thoughts and activities consume so much of your time that other aspects of your life and happiness are neglected. Being a workaholic means using work as a means of avoiding and dealing with other worries, which if resolved, would be likely to improve your happiness. Excessive eating similarly can be a negative way of managing personal worries.

There are a range of approaches available for coping with excessive destructive behaviour similar to dealing with alcohol abuse. Self-help groups such as Gamblers Anonymous, Sexaholics Anonymous and Overeaters Anonymous use programmes similar to the ones developed by AA. There are also professional programmes of assistance like detoxification programmes for abusers of alcohol and other drugs, generally accessible through hospitals or medical clinics.

There are two aspects of dependency that fall within the scope of this book. The first of these is how to relate to dependency (yours or your friend's) and the second is how to change some of the more common happiness-losing habits. Both these approaches may enable you to boost your happiness.

Not supporting the dependency

One of the difficulties with dependencies is deciding how you should react to them, whether they are in your family, your relationships, your friendships or yourself.

Dependency can be about excessive drug (legal or illegal) use. It can be about excessive and destructive behaviour which might include, not only the ones discussed above, but also the physical and verbal abuse of others.

TIPS

While the tips below are suggestions on how you might relate to someone else's dependency, they are also applicable to you, if you are dependent on a drug or a behaviour such as gambling.

- *Don't tell the dependent person their faults—they know them.*
  People who are dependent often do not wish to recognise it. To remind the smoker, the heavy drinker or the gambler of the consequences of their behaviour can, often as not, result in an aggressive outburst. It is a bit like saying, 'Try harder' or 'Snap out of it'—such suggestions tend to have the reverse effect. Reminding the person of their weakness tends to strengthen their belief in their own inadequacies, which in turn leads them to feel angry (and fearful) and to further pursue abusive behaviour to escape from these unhappy feelings.

- *Let them experience the consequences of what they are doing.*
  Sometimes, you, who are associated with the dependent person, are ashamed of their behaviour and seek to hide it from others. This happens if you pay the gambler's debts, hide the alcoholic's drinking from friends or buy the alcohol, or feed the overeater with the wrong but desired food. In these situations, it generally seems best if you allow the person to deal with the problems that follow from their dependency—such as fines, lack of money to go on outings, loss of job, or sickness, rather than try to solve their problems for them and by so doing support the dependency. This can be very difficult to do, as you probably love the other person and do not wish to see them hurt. Sometimes you may not wish their behaviour and your association with them to be revealed. In the end, however, it is only the dependent person who can change his or her behaviour. You can't make them, even though it is their change of behaviour that may make you more comfortable and increase your happiness. Allowing people to manage the consequences of their behaviour is one step towards them facing the results of their own actions.

- *Ensure that information on the particular difficulty is available.*
  While direct confrontation as described in the first point above is rarely successful, there is no need to shield people from information about their abuse. Information, for example, is often in the media, in news programmes, in the newspapers even in sports news, or in stories of people who have overcome similar problems. Again, to say to a dependent person, 'You should watch this,' may have the reverse effect. But there is no reason why you should not watch, listen to or read such messages, or for this information to be generally available in your house. Perhaps the dependent person will take notice too.

- *Understand when change might happen.*
  Most dependent people know the consequences of some of their behaviour. Smokers and alcoholics, for example, will generally be aware of the health-associated risks of their addiction. People with behaviour problems, such as gambling, will be usually aware of some of the effects their actions are having on their life. They are only likely to change, however, when they reach the point that they feel there is no alternative but to change. People who successfully break the cycle often themselves talk of hitting 'rock bottom' before they decide that change is the only option. Sometimes the decision to change will be a 'last straw' piece of information or event. It may not even be anything that someone else would think significant. For example, I know of a young woman who changed her vomiting bulimia-associated pattern when she discovered frequent vomiting would ruin her teeth (of which she was particularly proud).

- *Be supportive when asked.*
  A supporter's role when a decision to change is reached is to help with the actions the person wants to take in order to make the change. It is still important not to take over. Persons seeking change need to feel that this is what they want and that they are doing it. Support could be anything from taking them to the chemist shop to get nicotine patches, to driving them to the detox centre and staying with them while they are admitted, or

lending them the car to go to the AA meeting. Your own atten-
dance at a group such as Al-Anon, which is for those people
who have been associated with an alcoholic and who have
sometimes perhaps unwittingly supported the abuse (e.g. hid-
ing the problem from friends), might also be supportive.

- *Encourage hope.*

  Sometimes dependent people fear change more than living
  with the problem—'better the devil you know'. For dependent
  people to decide to change they need to feel there is some
  hope, that change is possible and that they are capable of it.
  Similarly, the supporter also needs to believe that there is hope.
  If you are a supporter, you are in a position to focus on other
  aspects of living. You can encourage the person to recognise
  the skills they have by drawing specific attention to them. You
  can help them develop new pursuits, new goals or revitalise old
  ones, or take on responsibilities that they can manage, in short
  anything which shows them they are worthwhile and capable.

- *See lapses as a sign of possible future success, rather than as a
  guarantee of sustained failure.*

  People who try to give up a destructive and debilitating habit
  may do so for variable lengths of time and on repeated occasions. It is important for both dependent people and supporters to remember that successive attempts are a sign of strong
  intentions to change and that success is often preceded by
  earlier failed attempts.

If you are able to support others who have these difficulties,
then you will find more happiness in your own life.

Louise's and Joe's story: Moderating an addiction to work

Joe and Louise had been married for a number of years. They
were both in their mid-forties and they had four children
spread through the early to late teenage years. Joe held a prominent position and was well known in his local community.
Over the early years of their marriage, Louise had strongly sup-

ported Joe's pursuit of his career. She also welcomed the lifestyle his high income gave them and enjoyed the prestige (outings and attention) that his position gave them.

The years passed and Joe became more and more involved in his work to the point where he was working seventy hours a week, and some weeks even eighty or ninety. He was obsessed with his job. As you can imagine, his family became estranged from him. Louise in particular found that she was now supporting his addiction by managing the family affairs and associated tasks. Finally she reached the point where she could no longer tolerate his behaviour. She told him she would leave if they didn't see a counsellor. The decision about how to respond to this ultimatum was partly taken out of Joe's hands as, in these days of rationalisation, he lost his job. They then both went to separate counsellors.

Joe had a good redundancy payment so he was able to take his time deciding his work future and his future relationship with his family. In the language of addictions, he had lost his fix (work) and was 'doing it hard'—he had gone cold turkey (total abstinence). With the support of his wife he re-identified his happiness goals and recognised the negative impact his addiction had had on them. As he reflected on his life, he realised that he was in fact good at many of the things he did in his previous employment—it was just that an excess of attention to them and associated peripheral aspects had begun to destroy the other parts of his life.

While he was initially devastated by his job loss, eventually he claimed that it was the greatest thing that had happened to him. He obtained employment in a non-profit organisation (success in his former position was in part measured by escalating profits), doing similar work but not at such a senior level as the position he had previously held. He was now able to balance his life between his work and his family.

Not all abuse problems will require the intervention of a health professional or rehabilitation unit. Smoking obviously injures our health, incurs large health costs, and harms others. Nevertheless there are many people who live with it. There are other non-treated forms of abuse—even some that may be affecting your life. At times you may wish to change these habits to improve your comfort and your control. The following exercise suggests some ways that enable you to make such changes.

Exercise 19: Steps for managing unwanted habits (minor dependencies)

The steps listed below include many strategies that have been used successfully to stop smoking, reduce alcohol consumption (confirmed and constant abusers of alcohol will need more special assistance), reduce caffeine, change your eating pattern (e.g. you may need to go on a special diet for health reasons such as high blood pressure). To undertake this exercise you need to choose a habit which is causing you to lose happiness—something which is making you uncomfortable— something which seems to be controlling you, rather than you controlling it—something which may bring future distress. This is not an exercise that you can give to someone else who you think would benefit from it! It only works if the person using the steps strongly wants to change.

1. Write down the reason that you want to change the habit. Reasons could include costs, health, performance at work, sport, or a combination of these. Be specific.

_____

_____

2. If reducing costs is the reason; work out how much you are spending now per day, per week, per month, per year. Work out how much you will save and what you will do with this saved money.

_____

_____

3. If you have nominated a health-related reason, describe what you want improved or the ill-health you are going to avoid by changing.

---

4. Go through any other reason in the same detail.

---

5. Take an average work day and go through it just documenting when you use the habit (e.g. 'Two cigarettes in bed before I get up,' or 'First cigarette is in the car on the way to work,' or 'I generally have a ciggy with my lunch'). Examine this average daily schedule to see when you are most likely to use your habit. These are the target times.

---

6. Check what is associated with these target times They may occur after a meal, or when you have a biscuit, or when you complete a piece of work, or when the tea is made, or before the television news, or whatever. You need to see if you can break the pattern by changing what you do. Changing what you have for lunch, avoiding that biscuit, playing with the computer rather than sitting in front of the television, finding something different to reward yourself with after a job is completed. It might be a glass of juice sipped slowly, enjoying every mouthful. The kind of patterns you will need to disrupt will depend on your particular daily schedule and the particular habit you want to change.

7. Temporarily avoid friends who are going to discourage you from the change or who merely by their presence might make it difficult. These people are not your supporters. On the other hand declare your intention to change to your supporters.

8. Find substitutes for your habit. You need to have something on hand to replace what you would ordinarily do with your habit. For smoking, this might be sugarless chewing gum, raisins, or chewing a toothpick; for drinking, this may be replacing the drinking time with an active but relaxing activity such as going for a walk; for a change in your eating pattern this may mean substituting an inappropriate food with one more consistent with the change you are seeking.

9. Draw the information worked out in the above steps into a daily schedule of not more than five points. Try to keep it simple and easy to follow.

_____

_____

_____

_____

_____

10. Follow the schedule. If you should slip on a part of it use this as a reminder to return to the path you have chosen and not as an excuse to abandon your plan. Try not to punish yourself with self-criticism for occasional lapses.

11. Nurture yourself in other respects. Choose a time to implement your plan which is not too stressful—it is rarely a good time to try to make a habit change if you are, for example, in the middle of a divorce settlement!

Regaining happiness after trauma

A trauma event can be anything from war to a serious accident, rape, being in a hold-up or being beaten. Such events will distress most people who experience them. Some consequences may include flashbacks in which the original event is 'relived' and the associated feelings experienced over again. Other forms of anxiety (e.g. being frightened of driving a car in the case of someone involved in a motor accident) may persist. Not everyone who experiences trauma experiences has these long-term effects.

To ease the immediate feelings of distress and in an effort to minimise the potential long-term consequences of trauma, counselling and critical incident debriefing procedures are often offered. While there is some professional argument about the effectiveness of different forms of debriefing, there are ways that friends and family can relate to victims that seem more supportive than others. These approaches are the ones that appear most likely to help the person to regain their previous level of wellbeing. And, as we have noted, our wellbeing, our happiness, is partly dependent on the wellbeing of others.

TIPS

These tips will help you relate to a friend or family member who has had a trauma experience, but they can also assist you if you have had such an experience.

- People will experience an event differently. A car accident, for example, will result in differing degrees of stress for different people. As a supporter, you cannot judge what is the 'right' amount of distress the person should feel.
- The reaction of trauma victims to alcohol will be heightened, and for this reason it is probably worthwhile encouraging them

to avoid it for a couple of days. (This is contrary to popular wisdom—such as having a brandy to 'steady the nerves'.)

- Immediate support can be given by driving the person home, staying with them and generally being available.
- Generally, it is not the technicalities of the event that a person needs to talk about for their emotional health, rather it is how they feel. Questions on the detail of the incident are often not helpful. It is more supportive to ask the person how they feel or felt—what it was like for them. They may need to tell their story a number of times, perhaps well beyond the first few days.
- Understand that their concentration and attention span may be decreased.
- It is common for people in these situations to become extra alert, to be fearful of everyday situations. For example, they may become extra wary of getting into a car, of crossing the road or going to a shop similar to the one where they saw a robbery. Your tolerance and understanding of this seemingly irrational fear will be helpful.
- The person may need to be reassured that the kind of distressing feelings described above are normal and common reactions to the experience they have had.
- People don't have to be in the frontline to experience these feelings, all they need to believe is that it could have happened to them. A person experiencing shock could have been someone in the back room when a shop is robbed, or may have been a witness to an accident but not personally involved.
- Recovery time is not easy to predict. Sometimes friends and family who have initially been comforting become impatient when, after a week or so, the person continues to experience the debilitating feelings. You need to be aware of this, and to be understanding if recovery is not as rapid as you would like.
- It is worth recognising that while a short temporary break from work or a reduction in workload may help initial recovery, generally, a return to regular routines as quickly as possible, including work, will help the person feel they are returning to normal living.

Happiness and grief

Even death can be seen as part of life.

FOR EXAMPLE

Uncle Charlie was about to leave this world. It was around five o'clock on a Saturday afternoon. The priest had arrived to administer the last rites. Before he could get going Uncle Charlie stopped him, demanding to know which horse had won the last race, and the results of his local football team's match!

George was on his deathbed surrounded by his relatives, grandchildren and great grandchildren, many of whom were praying for his recovery. George remarked: 'If you buggers would stop praying for me, I could die in peace.'

The most common form of personal loss is the death of a loved one. While you have or will recover from such experiences your recovery may be improved by knowing ways to cope with the feelings that emerge.

Living with losing someone

There is sadness when someone close to you dies. It is a natural feeling of loss and a reminder of your own mortality. To have such feelings is normal and ordinary. As time passes the feelings may seem to diminish in intensity and you usually get on with your life. There is, however, more than this to grief. You need to reach a position of balance in your life over your loss. The nature of your grief will also depend on the circumstances of the death, as well as on your own vulnerability.

Since the 1960s, particularly through the work of Elisabeth Kübler-Ross, ideas and information on relating to people who are dying and on our responses to death have become increasingly well known.

Stages, tasks or steps of grief

Acceptance

The most obvious and well-recognised first step in the grieving process is the acceptance of the death. This seems obvious enough, but is a step that is not always easily taken. In theatrical productions, a grieving person is sometimes shown as wanting to throw themselves into the grave. Less dramatically, you may find yourself expecting to see the dead person, perhaps at certain times such as coming home from work, or turning on the television set, or in the garden. In some societies, the display of the dead person's body until it deteriorates has the effect of showing that the person is no longer there.

FOR EXAMPLE

There are stories that Queen Victoria used to walk around Buckingham Palace talking to her deceased husband, Albert, several years after his death. Despite this she was quite mentally competent, though she did deeply miss her husband. She even introduced a type of mourning jewellery which was a black brooch made of ebony.

The acceptance of the fact of your separation from your loved one is generally said to be a necessary step in recovery from grief.

Expression of feelings

As with other traumatic events, the expression of the distress, anger and pain of your feelings seems to be an essential second step in healing. To hide or repress these feelings may delay or limit your return to more normal living. Thus to talk about your loss, to cry a little, to describe your feelings all seem helpful. In a sense it is similar to the views put forward elsewhere in this book with respect to pain. It is in recognising the presence of these feelings, rather than in trying to fight them off, that they are most likely to diminish.

In some cases, a third step involves adjusting to the dead person's absence in your life. This may mean taking on tasks that the other person did, such as household finances, washing, gardening, or cooking. It also has more profound implications. In an effective relationship, the other person may have been your best counsellor, your friend and your playmate. Similarly, your opportunity to provide support in these roles to the other person has also gone. Living with these changes may require a change in how you see yourself. Perhaps successfully completing this third step comes with doing some of the new tasks once the responsibility of the other person, and enhancing your feelings of self-worth by learning new skills.

Relating to the person who has died

Grief counsellors sometimes see the last step as placing the dead person in some appropriate emotional way in your memory and moving on with your life. Although, Phyllis Silverman at Harvard Medical School emphasises 'maintaining your history and connections with past, including your relationship with the dead person.'[10]

These views lead to a particular perspective on grieving which sees maintaining a bond with the dead person as an important task rather than disconnecting. This is about finding ways of living with the dead. While this may sound a little strange or macabre, it isn't. It is about using ways of thinking of the dead person, such as the way they may react to a current situation, the advice they may give, knowing whether they would enjoy the situation, or how they would handle it.

FOR EXAMPLE

Even now I can recall opinions and views of my long-deceased grandfather with whom I grew up. He had a laconic but accepting view of life illustrated in his stories. He used to tell me about the only time he ever went to see Don Bradman bat. The great man made a duck.

Coping with loss means bringing something of your loved one's attitudes and views into a personal, family or group context. For some people this will mean remembering the person in some spiritual—not necessarily religious—sense. Silverman emphasises the ritual part of this. In essence, you need to make meaning of the loss; once the bereaved person has reached this point, the grief can be considered to have stabilised but not to have disappeared. In this way, the dead person remains a part of the living person's life. It is consistent with the notion of your connectedness with others expressed in Principle 5. You establish and retain thoughts, concepts and images from those with whom you have been intimately related.

Coping with loss means bringing something of your loved one's attitudes and views into a personal, family or group context. From the point of view of our happiness perspective (*comfort*, *creativity* and to some extent our *control*) there are three positive features of such a position. The first is that it encourages continued access to the resources of the dead person. This can help you in your life performances (at work, home, or play). The second is that it can also help you to accept a changed relationship, without the kind of denial and potential distress that may develop from views that suggest you should disconnect. Third, it can help you see your own eventual death in a less disturbing light, thus decreasing anxiety and enhancing your sense of purpose in life (to connect with others, to share, to make stories together, to participate in community activities).

TIPS

The tips on grieving that follow combine the different views expressed above. They are written for you as a person grieving.

- Accept that you may need to grieve in ways different from others. How you choose to grieve needs only to be a way appropriate for you.
- Organise or be part of a farewell. Sometimes funerals can serve this function. There can be other rituals too which recognise the person's previous presence and provide visible signs of departure. Burning candles or making a small shrine are two examples of such rituals. Different cultures will have other rituals.
- Recognise that grieving is a commonly experienced process and that the expression of sadness and loss is both normal and necessary. Be ready to share your own concerns. Showing and talking about your feelings is an important step.
- As soon as possible, take up some of the tasks, jobs or roles formerly done by your loved one.
- Refer to the dead person for advice or comment if you are comfortable with this. Of course, if you didn't take their advice (or if it was usually bad advice) when they were living, there is absolutely no reason to take it when they are dead!
- Remember to incorporate in your life the gifts (certain skills, knowledge, types of jokes, sayings, beauty, attitudes or beliefs) that the dead person has left for you.

Summary

You have learnt:

- how addictions to legal or illegal drugs and other excessive behaviours (too much gambling, work or sex), diminish your chances of achieving your happiness goals.
- how you can assist friends and loved ones whose life is controlled by their problem habit.
- what steps you can take to remove your own unwanted

habits, such as stopping smoking, or reducing your alcohol or caffeine consumption.

- what you can do to assist yourself, a friend or partner who has had a traumatic experience.
- what you can do for yourself and how you can support others, when you or they are experiencing grief.

PRINCIPLE 7
LEARN HOW TO CHANGE YOUR MIND (AND HOW YOU FEEL)

Recognising that you may need to change the way you think about a particular job, person or circumstance may be the first step to change. However, it is sometimes difficult to replace the old way of thinking with a new approach. You may need to learn ways of making suggestions to yourself (and others) that are fruitful.

Ideas open to change

If you were born with a long nose like Cyrano de Bergerac, there is really little, except for plastic surgery, you can do to change it, though you may be able to alter the significance you give it in the way you see yourself—perhaps by valuing other attributes you may have, or by 'making light' of this aspect of your appearance. Your happiness in part relies on your acceptance of circumstances you cannot change.

A key issue, which affects whether you can change your mind, is what you *believe* is unchangeable and inevitable and what you believe is not.

At the heart of this distinction is your view of inheritance and the influence of your life circumstances. Can beliefs be inherited? If we are on shaky ground when we say of the young child that 'he has his father's mouth' (it may be more like his maternal great grandmother's, for all we know), then we are on even shakier ground when we say, 'he has his father's temper' (he may, but he could have learnt it rather than inherited it). Nonetheless, it is clear that while you have a whole range of inherent characteristics and abilities, you are also partly what you have learnt.

You are more likely to be able to change the ideas you have gained from this second source of influence (the learning provided by your teachers and your experiences). Thus your view of what will improve your appearance, or what will give you relief from stress, or what you like to eat, may all, along with other attitudes, be open to change.

To become happier you may need to change your mind. This can mean changes to your ideas of how to do things, to your ideas on what makes other people 'tick' and to your ideas on what is important. Changing your mind in this way can lead to recovery from emotional distress, or to an enhancement of performance.

Similarly, changing the way you feel about a situation, an attribute, or a future possibility can lead to wiser actions or choices—ones more likely to improve your opportunities and your wellbeing.

Changing an idea or feeling

Some ways of thinking become so powerful that to unlearn them can prove difficult. When most people believed the world was flat, clear reasoning alone was not sufficient to convince even well-known scholars to shed their long-held idea and embrace the new concept (the world is round). They needed a lot of evidence to build up to a point when they felt they could no longer deny the new possibility. Mentally things had to become so unbalanced, so dissatisfying, that they could no longer live comfortably with the old concept. It is a bit like that with us.

If you have thought for many years that the best way to get people to like you is to give in to them, or if you believe that if you don't complain loudly people won't change what they do, or if you judge that some form of punishment is the best way to change a child's undesirable behaviour, *then* it is going to take a lot of evidence to change the way you think—to sufficiently unbalance your view that it becomes too uncomfortable to hold. You are likely to grab hold of any exception you notice that supports your long-held position, so that you can maintain your favoured views.

There is a way around this difficulty. The strategy is not to reject outright the original view, but rather to say that other approaches will also be helpful. When you do this you tend to be adding ideas—you can focus on the new approach without rejecting the original one.

FOR EXAMPLE

You can say to yourself with respect to child-rearing practices, 'I am going to find opportunities to praise my child's good behaviour' rather than stressing their bad behaviour. Note you are not arguing that your original view, 'punishment is important', is wrong. You are adding to your options and looking for a chance to apply this extra strategy.

It is worthwhile remembering that the same principle applies when relating to others. In other words it might be far easier and more fruitful to persuade someone to try a new approach rather than tell them their present way of doing things is wrong.

This is not the only way to modify the way you think or feel. One of the most effective methods you can use to change or influence your own mind, or the minds and feelings of others, is to make and offer suggestions. Suggestions are especially likely to influence the way you feel and by this means change your attitudes and what you do.

They are likely to be more productive in some situations than others.

Circumstances for effective suggestions

Traditionally practitioners of hypnosis for clinical, health, or performance purposes describe our unconscious as the nine-tenths of the iceberg that lies under the surface. Whichever way you look at your mind, there are large chunks of mental resources and mental activity that you are not using at any particular time. But what you are unconscious of can become a conscious thought. You can, for example, remember a forgotten event by noticing something you associate with a past experience. What was unconscious becomes conscious.

FOR EXAMPLE
The smell of a bush, or flower, brings to mind a childhood picnic. You hear a piece of music and remember your first dance, your first date or the time you burnt the roast while listening to the music!

Suggestions can be like this—registered unconsciously but later influencing how you feel and think. It is commonly accepted that suggestions made to a person experiencing hypnosis are more likely to influence their feelings and actions than suggestions made in ordinary circumstances. Sometimes the person can be consciously aware of suggestions made during hypnosis and sometimes not.

Hypnosis is not a state of being asleep or unconscious—it is more like daydreaming. Hypnosis is not a state of being asleep or unconscious—it is more like daydreaming. Suggestions seem to be more readily taken on board by unconscious processes when you are in this state. Daydreaming is something you do naturally. A common experience is to be driving a car and not having recalled where you have been driving; another is to go 'off with the fairies' in the middle of a meeting and lose track of the conversation. You are more susceptible to suggestions when you are in such a trance-like state.

The principles used in hypnosis can be used to your advantage. Suggestions (even those of which you are aware) can further your goals. These principles of hypnosis have originated in your daily living experiences; they have generally been identified, adapted, refined and used by hypnotherapists rather than being invented by them. Dale Carnegie's famous book *How to Win Friends and Influence People* uses many of the same principles. Advertising firms also use similar techniques in their efforts to persuade you to change your mind.

TIPS

Suggestions can best hit the mark:

- when you are most receptive, that is, when you are in a state similar to daydreaming.
- when they fit your current views of yourself, others, and the world, or at least are not contrary to them (and are consistent with your happiness goals). In the example on child-rearing (page 000), the change you make to the way you behave towards your child is not about fundamental principles—you want your children to become well-adjusted adults regardless of the methods you are using in raising them—the change is about your ideas on how that might be done.
- if the suggestion is indirect or implied, rather than obvious. When this happens the suggestion can be responded to unconsciously without you needing to be aware of the 'message'.
- when they are contained in stories (including those used in everyday conversation), in film and advertising.

Obviously not all these conditions need be present for any one suggestion, or set of suggestions, to be effective, though usually a couple would be required.

You need to consider how you can apply suggestions to yourself, as well as to others, when that is appropriate, and how you can accept, or if necessary guard against, their impact on you when they are used by others.

Always remember that there are instances when you may want to avoid changing your mind.

In making suggestions to yourself and others, you are trying to create messages that will lead you (and others) to behave in a desired way.

To learn how your thinking and feelings can be influenced, it is worth looking at how suggestions can be made.

Repeated exposure

Perhaps the most obvious fact about suggestions is that their effectiveness increases with repetition. Advertisers use this in their slogans such as: 'Ah, Bisto!' and 'Beanz Meanz Heinz'. Who in the world cannot recognise the shape of a traditional Coca-Cola bottle? Learning by heart is not only a principle of general learning, but one that can be applied to suggestions. It is interesting to note that companies like Coca-Cola continue to advertise persistently and heavily, because they know that to let up will lead to a fall off in sales, even for their well-known product. Nagging can work! This is especially true when it is done positively. It is not true if done negatively and contrary to the person's view of how things should be: a teenager's resistance to constant parental criticism about an untidy room can turn into World War III in a matter of days.

If you want to influence your children—won't it make you happier if they develop more in the way you would like?—then you will want them to be exposed most to the range of suggestions and messages that you favour. To what extent is this happening? Can you change the circumstances of your lives (and theirs) to exert greater influence, *control*, if that's what you want? (What can you do to influence television viewing habits? Sit with them; jointly select programmes; arrange alternative activities; discuss what makes some programmes more enjoyable than others are just a few possibilities.)

There are other applications of the exposure suggestion rule. In a factory, for example, instructions on how to use a machine safely are not much use tucked away in the drawer of the supervisor's bench.

The repetition of suggestions is a practice that will work best when the suggestions are ones that the recipient can accept both consciously and implicitly (unconsciously) as valuable. Repeated self-exposure to personally beneficial suggestions is also important. The more frequently you offer yourself suggestions about your own worth or value (e.g. 'I am a someone who will cope in most situations') the more likely are you to feel and to behave in that way. Of course the suggestions need to be within the realms of possibility. For the vicious criminal, Hannibal Lecter (*Silence of the Lambs*), to keep telling himself that he is going to become a leading character on children's television would seem unrealistic!

> The more frequently you offer yourself suggestions about your own worth or value, the more likely are you to feel and behave in a positive way.

Emotional appeal

It is sometimes easier to get a person to respond to a suggestion because of its emotional appeal and only later to explain the wisdom of making such a choice. It is a technique often favoured by advertisers. In general, advertisers appeal to strong emotions. Thus we are shown a family carrying on successfully on the proceeds of life insurance after the death of one or other of the parents. The appeal to your feelings is paramount and any logical argument about the relative merits of taking out life insurance as opposed to any other method of catering for an unforseen future is at best in the background. This type of suggestion is captured in the old story about the minister's sermon; he had written on the edge of one particular text, 'point weak, shout like hell'. A similar story is commonly told about lawyers who try first to get a jury to feel sympathy towards their client before producing any argument to persuade them of their client's innocence. It is also the case that stronger emotions take precedence over weaker ones, though the kind of emotions felt most strongly will not always be the same for each of us.

You probably have experienced situations where others have appealed to your feelings of importance—'You will really have made the grade when you have completed that report' or 'I would have thought that someone with your knowledge of business would have seen the value of this insurance policy'; to your feelings of physical prowess—'With further training you'll be one of the fittest in the team'; to your feelings of attractiveness—'There is no doubt that when you are all cleaned up with your hair washed you look pretty good—I bet the girls will beat a path to your door!'

These emotional appeals contain the following indirect suggestions:

- finish the report, get on with it (from the supervisor);
- buy this policy (from the insurance representative);
- do more training (from the coach);
- make sure you always keep clean (from mum to son).

There are two ways of looking at suggestions aimed at your emotions. One is to ensure that if you are a recipient of such a suggestion you do not let it lead you away from your happiness goals. The other is to consider whether you can or *should* use them, and if you do, how you might go about that.

Exercise 20: Recognising suggestions based on emotional appeal

1. Work out and write down briefly three suggestions that could get you to do something by appealing to you through your feelings.

_____

_____

_____

2. What attributes are being appealed to—appearance, status, skill level, freedom?

_____

_____

3. Now consider your partner, or a friend, and write down three suggestions that you could make to them, appealing to their emotions. You may find this easier than writing suggestions for yourself. (This is because we are sometimes not fully aware of our own emotional buttons.)

_____

_____

_____

4. You can also ask whether the suggestions you have made for your partner/friend are fair. Not all emotional appeals are wrong, not all are right. It depends on whether the reasoning that accompanies them is sound—unlike the minister's sermon.

5. Another twist to this exercise is to have your friend/partner complete the same little task. When you compare your results with theirs you can see how similar (or how different) they are and what you can each learn about yourselves through the comparisons.

It is important to be aware of the suggestions that appeal to you most and to avoid immediately responding to such suggestions, even though you feel strongly inclined to do so. In the long run, such suggestions may make sense, but your response

should come after you have delayed your initial reactions and
shelved your immediate feelings.

Putting things in the best light

When you put something in a positive way, you can make a
creative new suggestion. You can view the world pessimisti-
cally—the glass is half empty instead of the glass is half full.
Or optimistically—get up in the morning and say, 'Good
morning, God' instead of 'Good God! Morning!' In the jargon of social science this is called reframing.

Politicians are often considered the experts of this creative
art: a broken-down road becomes 'the beginning of a new
freeway', or a downturn in the economy is 'the reason why
we need tax reform'. While these examples may seem a little
cynical, reframing is an important way of making positive
suggestions. To reframe is to change your mind about a set of
circumstances.

It is often better to see a current set of business circumstances as a challenge and an opportunity rather than a difficulty or a problem. This is not just being tricky with words. It
is usually true that a situation that may require problem-
solving will also often provide an opportunity for new learning. Similarly you can suggest to yourself (or others) that a
personal problem is a challenge rather than a difficulty. When
you do this you give yourself a better chance of coming up
with a creative option. The alternative, wallowing in the problem, usually limits your likelihood of reaching further happiness goals in whatever part of your life you are experiencing
the challenge.

The kinds of life issues where positive suggestions are
helpful can range from the mundane to the dramatic. You can
suggest that sweeping the floor or washing the clothes are

opportunities for exercise, for creating order in the house, for contributing to family hygiene, and for appreciating your living environment and its appearance. You can suggest that by preparing a garden bed, servicing the car, or recycling the rubbish, you are contributing to your health, your future creative opportunities, your continued mobility and perhaps even offering something to the future of life on our planet! You can suggest that a broken friendship or a lost promotion are opportunities to re-appraise your life and to celebrate new beginnings.

Positive suggestions enable you to behave more constructively, more creatively. They can help you to live more comfortably with the ups and downs of life and to better control your reactions to changes in your life.

Realistic optimism is the only game in town. Anything else will detract from your happiness. This is a state of mind well worth cultivating.

Exercise 21: Recognising opportunities

1. Find yourself a pen, a spare notebook, and a quiet place to work.
2. Take three current life issues that you consider are problems in your life at home or at work. Describe them and then reframe them in a positive way.
3. What future actions do these reframed descriptions suggest?
4. Take two complaints that your friend or partner has about circumstances in their lives. Reframe these views. What difference would these reframed views make to their lives?

You may find it easier to see how to improve another person's circumstances rather than your own. Perhaps if you can recognise their opportunities, you will be able to return to your issues and reframe them more easily, and reflect on them.

Jamie's story: Growing-up or growing-down?

Jamie was the first child of Jean and John. They had three other children all under five years old. Both parents were quite engaged with their children. John often spent time with their first-born in particular, reading stories to him and playing games.

When Jamie started school he was very reluctant to go—he cried frequently, wouldn't let his mother go and was clearly quite miserable. The school arranged for a school support person to visit Jamie's home, which was done after hours. Most of the conversation took place between the parents and the visiting counsellor.

During the course of their discussion John remarked that all he wanted was for Jamie to 'grow-up'. The counsellor used this opportunity to explore what they meant by growing-up and what kind of behaviour they thought of as 'growing-down'. What type of behaviour leads a child away from becoming more independent and mature? In thinking of things this way John and Jean saw that growing-up is when you take more responsibility and growing-down is when you take less.

The couple then worked out that for Jamie growing-up activities could be: making his own lunch, choosing his clothes for school, or his father taking him to school but not walking him all the way in. These were explained to Jamie as things that were showing how grown-up he was becoming. Similarly, because he was 'big', he was given responsibility for assisting his little sister to have a bath. A glitch in this process occurred when Jamie's teacher encouraged him to bring his Teddy to school. In some situations this would be fine but for Jamie it was a growing-down activity. Nevertheless, this issue was minor and the overall approach worked well.

Jamie thus became more in control of his environment and a participant in what was happening. He was still allowed to see himself as part of his family (he had their picture in his work book) and he was less inclined to feel separated from them by school.

In this story a variety of suggestions were used including the emotional appeal to Jamie of being big and grown-up. The idea of growing-up provided an opportunity to reframe Jamie's behaviour to include a range of independent actions.

Getting agreement

Principle 7 can apply to others as well as to yourself. It is quite legitimate to want to change someone else's mind or how they feel. In getting a person to agree with an idea, a number of statements are made, which the person agrees with, before a final suggestion is made. The listener, reader or viewer is encouraged to say 'yes' so many times that by the time the suggestion is made the expectation is to say 'yes' again.

To take a simple example: Have you ever been out on a really hot sunny day? (yes) Have you ever felt so warm that you have perspired? (yes) At times like this I bet you found you became thirsty? (yes) Sometimes so thirsty that I suspect your mouth became dry? (yes) In fact, aren't you starting to feel thirsty now? (yes) Of course, this last question is the suggestion.

It is fairly easy to see how this approach can be applied in advertising or in other situations like political campaigns where persuasion seems important.

In daily living, too, you can lead someone to accept the worth of a suggestion you wish to make.

FOR EXAMPLE

When trying to persuade a child to take swimming lessons: 'You like going outside don't you? Do you enjoy playing with friends? Would you like to play with them on the beach with a ball or a Frisbee? It would be fun to do that in the shallows wouldn't it? Your friends (who can swim) can do that in deeper water can't they? You could join them there if you could swim better, couldn't you?'

Similar approaches can be used on a whole range of topics for children and adults, providing you adjust the language and style to suit the circumstances.

In your exchanges with others at work or at home there may be times when you experience this tactic. It is something to be aware of, something to guard against, if the consequences of accepting the suggestion lead you away from your goals. The first indication that something like this is occurring is when you find yourself agreeing with statements that must be true.

Trying harder

Be careful of situations where you try to make a direct suggestion, or will yourself to do something. This is usually a very unsuccessful way of trying to change your mind.

Have you ever tried willing yourself to sleep; or tried forcing yourself not to feel excited, worried or anxious when you were already starting to feel that way; or tried to stop your heart from racing? The effect is often the reverse of the one you want; you become even more wide awake, you get more worried, or your heart seems to race even faster.

When you are feeling excited or angry, awake or tired, trying to stop the feeling by force will often only have the opposite effect.

In hypnosis, phrases like 'the harder you try the more difficult you will find it' are sometimes used. For situations where you are experiencing feelings, such as being excited, or angry, awake or tired, trying to stop the feeling by force will often only have the opposite effect. On a long drive at night, for example, you may need to take rests rather than try to will yourself awake.

FOR EXAMPLE

Try hard *not* to think of a beach with golden sands, lapping waves and seagulls flying above. Now, stop thinking about it!

It is important to know that suggestions to try harder don't work. When you (or others) are becoming uncomfortable and losing control of your feelings, it is often no use telling yourself (or others) to 'snap out of it' or 'take control and pull yourself out of it' or 'stop feeling sorry for yourself'. More creative actions and suggestions are required. If you are feeling anxious several days before a job interview, don't try to will yourself to be calm. You need to approach the situation in a less direct way by positively paying attention to other events around you (e.g. the garden, the layout of houses in the street, television) or by distracting yourself with some attention-demanding activity (e.g. a computer game, a crossword puzzle, playing or listening to music).

If, as sometimes happens, the negative thoughts make it difficult to concentrate on other, even non-demanding, situations, then physical activity such as going for a walk, playing a game of tennis, or gardening might prove helpful. Even *accepting the presence of unpleasant thoughts* may prove more helpful than trying to force them away—they will go away of their own accord. When you experience pain or worry, it is sometimes less stressful to recognise the presence of unpleasant pain or feelings with self-talk such as 'I've coped before', 'I'll manage', than it is to try to force it to go by saying to ourselves 'This is awful', 'I cannot manage it', 'I can't stand it', 'It must go away.'

How time lags (or flies)

Have you ever noticed how long it seems to take when you are waiting in a queue to buy something, waiting at a bus stop after you just missed a bus, waiting in the bank to do a simple transaction or waiting in traffic when you are already ten minutes late for that meeting? Your judgment of how long something takes depends on the circumstances and, more importantly, on the suggestions you make to yourself at the time.

In your daily life, you can feel that pleasant experiences pass too rapidly if you focus on their duration. You are better off to accept the enjoyable event rather than evaluating it and hoping for more.

If you are giving yourself suggestions like, 'I'll never get there', 'The film will be over by the time I arrive' or 'I'll be in trouble when I get back to work', then you are likely to see the time passing even more slowly. To change how you feel about the situation it is usually better to make suggestions more accepting of the situation, such as 'I'll get there eventually', 'I won't miss much of the film and I'll be able to pick it up easily anyhow' or 'even if the boss doesn't understand, I'll live.' There are even more positive ways of viewing a period of waiting: 'I'll just check out my plans for the weekend'; 'It's pleasant to rest here'; or 'I'll turn on the radio and catch the news.'

Sometimes when you are engrossed in or enjoying an experience, time seems to be passing rapidly. Hypnotherapists sometimes use this capacity to suggest that even unpleasant experiences can seem to last for shorter and shorter periods.

In your daily life, you can feel that pleasant experiences pass too rapidly if you focus on their duration—'I wish this wouldn't stop', 'I wonder when I can experience this again.' As with negative experiences, you are better off accepting the enjoyable event rather than evaluating it and hoping for more. Although when you have a negative experience, self-talk such as 'this will pass' or 'it won't last forever' may ease the passage of such unwanted feelings.

So can you see how your view of time can be adapted to assist you to live in greater harmony with your happiness goals? Changing how you feel and think is a key ingredient of a happy life.

Summary

You have learnt that:

- for a suggestion to stick, constant repetition and exposure are necessary. That is why advertisers keep showing the same product continually even though it is well known. It works.
- suggestions which are connected with a strong emotion tend to be effective. 'If you want to be considered attractive or intelligent, then follow this suggestion.'
- positive suggestions which put troubling circumstances in a good light as challenges or opportunities are more likely to lead to positive and helpful results, than are negative suggestions. This is called *reframing*.
- you need to be alert to being 'led down the garden path' by a series of obviously true questions or statements to an idea or action you may or may not want.
- suggestions that urge you to try harder when you are facing problems, obstacles or worries do not generally work. You are usually better off focusing on something else and accepting the difficulty rather than fighting it in your head.
- an experience may appear longer or shorter depending on how you talk to yourself about it. Pleasant experiences can seem to finish too quickly while unpleasant ones seem to last.
- it is through acceptance, undertaking alternative activities, or by putting a positive construction on a stressful situation that you are most able to diminish its impact.

PRINCIPLE 8
USE THE IDEAS OF GREAT TEACHERS

The ideas of great spiritual teachers can provide unifying strategies that overarch other happiness principles and focus on core aspects of your life. Concepts and philosophies that have stood the test of time have these centre-of-life features.

Spiritual teachers and happiness

Spiritual teachers seek to speak to your internal life through rules and practices for your body and mind. They talk about managing your emotions, feelings and basic appetites, ways of 'right' thinking, and kinds of self-awareness. Through stories, parables and suggestions they tap into your creative learning. Similarly, spiritual teachers tell you what they think you should do when you are involved with outside circumstances. You can look to them for guidance on how to relate to others, what to do in times of crisis and loss, and how you should heal yourself from unhappiness. So the ideas of spiritual teachers, sometimes expressed in religious creeds, can be applied to most of the issues considered in this book.

Of course not everyone supports religious messages. Karl Marx described religion as 'the opium of the people'. His view was that religion 'drugged' poor people into accepting their lot in the world and not fighting for their rights. These days there are many examples of religious leaders arguing on behalf of disenfranchised people. Church leaders in Australia have supported Aborigines politically, bishops in South America have been outspoken in their support of the needs of the poor of their countries, and Bishop Tutu entered the public arena on behalf of truth and justice for black South Africans.

More relevant to the concerns of this book is the criticism of religion which has been around for most of this century and is captured in the oft-quoted phrase said to apply to believers—namely that they are looking for the 'pie in the sky when they die'. It is a view that suggests believers are just as self-centred in their behaviour as non-believers since they (believers) are also acting to receive a reward; it's just that it is delayed. Like the opinion expressed by Marx this one too is a bit too broad and overly simple. As with most generalisations the problem is that it may be partially true for some people, but rarely true for everyone.

Indeed, the ideas and practices of religion seem more likely to lead us away from selfish behaviour than towards it. And even if the motive is not pure (there's a basket of goodies waiting for you when you die) this book is more concerned with what you can derive from various religions for your daily living, rather than in religious theory.

Common religious ideas

Spiritual teachers advise people how to behave through sets of rules and different forms of religious practice. In the Christian and Judaic traditions, the rules include the Ten Commandments; Buddhists refer to the Middle Way with its Eight-Fold Path; followers of the Islamic religion are guided by the teachings of the Koran; and hundreds of years before Christendom, many Chinese were guided by Lao-tse and Taoism (wise sayings about the truth).

In examining ideas from religion you are really considering strategies for moving forward in your life which combine inside intentions with outside actions.

While I am not promoting any particular religious belief, some of the understandings and practices discussed here *are* spiritual, in the same sense that wonder and awe at the continuing mysteries of ourselves and the universe are spiritual. The teachings we'll explore are common ones that are consistent with at least some professional opinions. Of course professional opinions themselves are not uniformly agreed anyhow!

Blame, forgiveness and reparation

Blaming others and encouraging their feelings of guilt or feeling guilty yourself is not a recipe for *comfort*. Feelings of guilt can cause you to lose *control* in an outburst of anger. Guilt can influence you to be inactive because you are afraid of making further mistakes and feeling even guiltier. These emotional reactions are well known. Perhaps you have experienced them.

Forgiveness is one way to help you overcome guilt. It is a philosophy taught by many religions, and it is formally recognised in the practices of the Catholic Church through the forgiveness extended to the parishioner in confession (now referred to as 'reconciliation'). It is a practice well expressed in prayer and contemplation where you may ask to be forgiven for your own misdeeds to the same extent that you forgive those who act against you. This is the main message of *The Lord's Prayer*. In the Buddhist and Hindu traditions you may avoid increasing your bank of misdeeds by your forgiveness of others. Similarly, many religious ideologies urge you not to judge others.

Non-judgmentalism and forgivingness can be difficult attitudes to adopt. They often seem contrary to much popular culture and often run against your feelings and beliefs about justice, revenge, reward, punishment and fairness. To forgive a particular person but not their actions can, however, be consistent with the spirit of the religious position—just as you can say to a young child, 'I love you but I hate that horrible noise you are making.' Additionally forgiveness should not be confused with allowing someone else to abandon their responsibility. While forgiveness doesn't mean revenge, it also doesn't mean 'letting off' someone from their responsibilities.

Allowing someone to experience the consequences of their behaviour is a difficult act of love—probably more loving than unjustifiably protecting them from the results of their actions. In a way, you are forgiving them for behaving inappropriately before it even happens!

FOR EXAMPLE

Let your child experience the consequence of eating all the biscuits—there are no more until the next pay day. Allow the young person determined to experience feeling drunk, the experience of an unsympathesised hangover. Even if you are going somewhere as a couple, allow your partner (or it could be you!) to experience the consequences of being late for the film, party, or train, without hassling them about time.

It can be just as difficult for you to forgive yourself as it is to forgive others. Self-forgiveness requires us to relinquish guilt but not responsibility.

The twin notions of forgiveness (self and others) and acceptance of responsibility are psychologically sound attitudes which will support your emotional wellbeing.

Steps for forgiveness

Forgiveness of yourself or others is not always easily come by. You may need to approach it little by little. To approach forgiveness head-on may be unproductive.

- *Focus on the needs of others.* Look for what might be of use to them—ask them if they want it—provide it if you can. By looking at others you are redirecting your attention away from yourself and making yourself more ready to adopt a mental attitude of forgiveness. This attitude is also one which helps you to be less blaming of yourself for your own mistakes.

- Ask your personal inner adviser for help, pray or use *affirmations* such as, 'I can accept it if so-and-so (someone you feel has done you wrong) becomes happier' or in forgiving yourself, 'I generally do the best I can' or 'I am learning how to forgive myself' or as a loving uncle used to say to me, 'You're as good as the next bastard!'

- At times you may even need to work on *overcoming your negative feelings* towards someone else before you can even spiritually or mentally wish them well. Usually dealing with your negative feelings towards others is achievable when you come to terms with your own problems. When, for example, you look forward to future possibilities rather than continuing to hurt yourself because you didn't get that promotion, or because someone criticised your appearance or your behaviour. It may also mean doing, at least temporarily, a bit of self-nurturing.

- If you can manage it, *reparation* (repairing damage) is an effective forgiveness tool. It is one of the last steps advocated in AA recovery programmes. It is also used by some counselling programmes.[11] At the personal level self-nurturing is a way of self-reparation—seeking to fix-up the damage you have done to yourself through self-blame. More arduous is making reparation to another person for the harm you may have caused them. It could mean, for example, asking your parents or your children to forgive you for a part you may have played in some aspect of their lives which gave them some unhappiness. Even more difficult is asking someone to forgive you because you have condoned behaviour which has caused you unhappiness. If the problem is alcohol, the non-alcoholic partner may need to ask the alcoholic one to forgive them for supporting the addiction. A very tough call, but a particularly meaningful communication. Sometimes it could mean doing acts of reparation, such as performing a household chore for that relative with whom you had that argument.

Reparation is not only a Christian notion, it also forms part of the Hindu, Buddhist and Muslim traditions. G. I. Gurdjieff, gleaning ideas from Asia and the Middle East, became a renowned spiritual teacher living in Moscow in the first half of the twentieth century. He talked about the need to repair the past, but not to indulge in self-recrimination.[12]

Surrender (acceptance) and freedom

Surrender is often a prominent feature of religion. Jesus Christ asked his disciples to leave all and follow him. In India, people often devote their lives to understanding a guru's teachings. Surrendering to the will of Allah, in the Muslim faith, or the teachings of Buddha is highly valued in each respective tradition. Very loosely the idea of surrender is seen as a way to become a devout practitioner of the faith. It is seen as focusing you on 'right' behaviours and avoiding ones (selfishness, anger, greed, blaming others) which will lead you away from your spiritual goals. For your purposes, you can think of surrender as avoiding actions and thoughts that will lead you down the path of unhappiness. Surrender yourself to constructive thoughts and behaviour.

Sometimes the idea of surrender is criticised by those who desire social change. They see surrender as passive acceptance— as just a recipe for inactivity. This need not be so. Indeed change may be sought to better adjust the world to the will of a spiritual leader. At the worst extreme, history is littered with acts of violence done in the name of religion.

At a personal and more positive level you can act to improve a situation, because you are following a particular code—religious or otherwise. Help someone, share your resources with others, show friendship or give unconditional love. Surrendering to someone else's doctrine can be a form of active acceptance.

In my opinion that well-known religious exhortation, 'God give me the courage to change the things I can change, the serenity to accept the things I cannot change and the wisdom to know the difference,' has a sound basis in psychology. There is little doubt that by following such a code you can achieve greater internal *comfort*. You can feel that your actions better match your views. You can avoid the negative emotional consequences of continually wishing the world was different (the 'if-only-this-would-change' or 'I-wish-my-husband/wife/parent-were-like-so-and-so' type of thinking).

A common and natural fear is that, by surrendering or accepting, you let go of your freedom. Or to put it another way, you relinquish your capacity to personally decide what is right or wrong. In recent years, we've heard of young people who get themselves into religious groups and find themselves cut off from their families, and sometimes involved in practices which they don't actually support. There have also been incidents of obscure religious sects where the members have apparently voluntarily participated in mass suicides. In the broad sweep of religion, however, surrender doesn't mean losing touch with reality or subjecting yourself to practices inconsistent with your basic values.

A frequently expressed religious view of surrender is that it paradoxically leads to freedom. In this understanding, surrender means losing the unhappiness caused by your biological and psychological addictions. It means, for example, getting control of any problems you might have with your desire for food, sex, power or status. You are freer, in this view, if you are deciding what to do rather than being controlled by natural or social forces. If you are leading yourself to unhappiness through the way you manage your appetites, desires and aspirations then you may need to surrender to your values, rather than surrender to behaviour which leads to unhappiness. Another way of putting this is to say as Lao-tse says, 'The perfect man is selfless.' Such a person does not focus on ambition, security or personal needs.[13] How you might do this has been examined in several parts of this book. A programme for change is also suggested in the final exercise on page 231.

Gloria's story: Acceptance and new beginnings

Gloria and her husband Doug were what many people would consider a very successful couple blessed with the things many people wish for. By the time they had reached their mid-fifties, they had three very successful adult children with high status jobs. Doug had been a senior in a company for many years and could not be considered naive about financial matters. Gloria had been a pillar in the local community, well respected for her voluntary work and church activities.

Gloria approached a counsellor after they had lost the money that had been invested in a long established overseas company, which previously had a good reputation. Within the same timeframe Doug became unemployed. Gloria was endeavouring to support him emotionally, as well as herself recovering from the shock of these substantial losses. There was even a possibility of them having to sell their home. Gloria, whilst trying to be of help to her husband, could see that there was a limit to what she could do. She also had lost faith in her religion.

Gloria's counselling sessions consisted of long discussions about the important things in life. In some senses, she was resentful of her husband's participation in their changed circumstances.

After several sessions, she reached a point where she could forgive the somewhat unknown financial situation that caused the change to her life. She also found it possible to accept the new circumstances. Perhaps, most importantly, she began to regain her meaning in life by exploring how different religious traditions looked at life. Through these means she reached a better understanding of herself and a view which was different from her original catastrophic outlook—that everything was lost. As she started to rebuild her life she found she could assist her husband by just being available. Eventually he obtained some employment.

Gloria's attitude of acceptance and her capacity to generate new meaning for her life—she saw the importance of her former church activities; the contributions she could make to others; the connections she had maintained with her adult children; the joy she felt in her garden and her feeling of being at peace—all contributed to a new beginning and a way of feeling happy.

Life is a teacher

Many religious traditions take the view that life is a teacher. If you can learn from your mistakes, you can lead a better, more effective life. This belief is consistent with the kind of reasoning we looked at in Principle 7. It means regarding problems as challenges and opportunities to learn new life strategies to help you better achieve your goals.

Some spiritual teachers warn against living like a sleepwalker—acting out your life as if you were dreaming. It is psychologically the case that many of us do spend a good deal of our time 'living' in our heads.

This can occur when, for example, you consider another person's action not just for what it is, but for what it might mean to you for your future, or how it reflects on you or your loved ones, or how you might use it for your benefit. Thus you are focused internally, talking to yourself about the events that are happening rather than seeing them for what they are. It is possible to move through the world not noticing what is around you: the scenery, the traffic, the idea expressed by that person, or the breeze on your face.

To learn from your experiences you need to notice them. Sounds easy.

At times, you may become totally immersed in your thoughts of criticism, or personal desires before you realise it. Sometimes you can become so involved with your thoughts that you find it difficult to listen to another's. You interrupt them, or perhaps even more commonly, listen to your inner chattering and not to what the other person is saying.

When you do these things, you are not noticing what is going on around you, and, as well, you are often not recognising the nature of your own thoughts. So to learn from experience, you need to notice what is happening around you as well as be aware of the kind of thoughts you are having. It is often by becoming aware that you change your way of thinking or doing things and bring them more in-tune with what you value and with what you are seeking. The exercise which follows offers a number of suggestions which may help you to notice what is happening or, you could say, to be more attentive.

Exercise 22: Ways of paying attention

1. Try taking a short five-minute walk just using your senses and noticing what you can see, smell, hear or feel. If you find your mind straying onto the problems of the day or personal issues, or even onto positive thoughts such as your next holiday, just notice these thoughts and bring your attention to looking at the trees, the neighbour's garden, that new front fence, the smell of a fir tree, the birds chirping, and so on.

   Note that you are not trying to think about these things, to pass judgement on them, or to let them act as reminders of something you want to do. You are just trying to notice them. Over time you can gradually go on longer walks. This exercise is best done alone, and requires practice. If you are like me you may feel lucky if you get five or ten minutes of attending out of a half an hour's walk. You are not in the business, however, of making comparisons, such as saying yesterday's walk was better than today's. It is just a matter of taking each day as it comes.

2. When you are doing a mundane kitchen job, say washing up or sweeping the floor, pay attention to the task by looking for the crumbs, noticing how you are cleaning that plate or saucepan or where you need to sweep or whether you are leaning over too much and seeing if you can hold your body differently. A Christian saint, St Thérèsè of Lisieux, who is known as the 'Little Flower', lived her life paying attention to everyday jobs, and is reputed to have said that 'God walks among the pots and pipkins'(of the kitchen). Doing the ordinary well can be important.

3. To recognise the nature of your thoughts, you probably need to be able to describe them to yourself. You may, for example, be thinking critical thoughts about your new boss. You could say to yourself: 'I am thinking this way because I don't like the way he is taking status from me by making me defer to him for those jobs.'

   If you are angry with your partner for running late, you could describe the situation to yourself: 'I am feeling angry because I believe it is essential that we be on time,' instead of just fuming and being angry. Or, maybe when you see a pie in the shop window ten minutes after breakfast and feel you would like to have it, say to yourself: 'I am feeling hungry because my senses are telling me that pies are nice to eat, even though my senses are not telling me that I need the food.'

4. To practise recognising your thoughts, stop three times a day, for half a minute or two, and describe to yourself what you are thinking. This is not meant to be a tool with which to punish yourself. It is meant as an exercise to assist you to pay attention, which ultimately will help you to learn from experience.

And the whole damn thing

From the stories handed down by our ancestors to the efforts of scientists we continue to search for the meaning of life.

Our search probably begins when we are teenagers seeking to understand our living circumstances and then as adults seeking meaning for our present and future life.

While you often may try to hide from the uncertain knowledge about your existence by pushing it into the background and burning on vigorously in pursuit of career, pleasure, recreation or the accumulation of wealth, it is always there challenging the worthwhileness of what you do. Having a meaningful life is incredibly important. There is even a school of therapy called logotherapy which is based on giving meaning to your life.[14] Whether their views are accurate or mistaken, people who live life contentedly are often those who are satisfied with their understanding of it.

Giving meaning to life through your understanding of living, love and death can help you to feel that your activities have some purpose. A clear understanding of your purpose provides a base from which to further explore new ideas. An understanding of the role of love in your life, for example, can help you to be less confused in your relationships with others, not just with your partner. You can see more clearly what matters and can feel more satisfied that your actions are the right ones for you.

Understanding living

The unitary nature of life is a theme which runs through many approaches to spiritual living, especially in Eastern traditions. It is a view which suggests that you are part and parcel of everything else, that you are intimately interrelated with the world and that you can recognise aspects of yourself in other forms of life. It takes you away from seeing yourself as the centre of things. It helps you to see yourself as part of the web of life.

Your fear of others will diminish if you see in them some of the things you see in yourself. In counselling sessions, people often feel much better when they understand that they are not alone and that many others have had experiences and feelings similar to the ones they are having. Your attitude to the problems of living becomes more optimistic if you understand that you are related to others in many aspects of your intentions, purposes, worries and hopes.

This interrelated view of the world also stresses your connection with nature in general—your dependence, for example, on plants to give you food. It is expressed in the Native Americans' thanks to the buffaloes who gave up their lives to feed the tribe. Interdependence is central. What you do personally (e.g. depleting the ozone layer by using aerosol sprays, driving inefficiently or excessively, supporting the use of CO_2-producing power plants) can affect weather patterns, which can affect crops and stock, and therefore the income of farmers, and this may have drastic repercussions in Third World countries.

The sciences emphasise our position in the big picture. We now know:

- People are literally made of star dust—the origin of what makes up your body comes from the exploding stars of the expanding universe.
- All things, including you, are made up of particles or wave motions.
- Emptiness is most of everything, including you. You are related in this way to the wider universe.
- Explaining the development of life on earth requires more than the theory of evolution. It includes an in-built tendency towards organisation. In other words, the way life is, is more than chance.

In some ways the paradoxes of contemporary science appear more mystical than some religious ideas. Leaving aside scientific complexities it is obvious that scientific opinions point to your interrelatedness and interdependence with the rest of existence. Stuart Kauffman, a biologist who also studies physics, has written a book called *At Home in the Universe*.[15] His central theme is that in evolution there is a tendency towards order and organisation that precedes Darwin's theory of the survival of the fittest. He focuses on the importance of design and gives a lesser role to chance. Look around you and notice the relationship which is developing between some spiritual views and some aspects of contemporary science. There are more scientists, such as Paul Davies, Fritjof Capra and Frank Tipler, writing about spiritual ideas, even ones as abstract as immortality. Even the famous agnostic scientist, Stephen Hawking, talks about the mind of God.

Feeling connected with others and related to the world is important. As you increase your understanding of yourself, your place in the world and your interrelatedness to others, so you enhance your prospects of feeling comfortable with your life.

REFLECTION
- Spend five minutes for each of the next five days contemplating someone else's actions and try to work out what is motivating them. To what extent are their motives similar to yours?
- Spend five minutes for each of five days contemplating the stars at night—just wondering and looking.

Love

Have you ever heard someone say that they need two partners, 'one for lust and one to dust'? Though a joke, this sentiment is glib and it certainly doesn't express love. You have probably heard the saying that 'love is giving and not counting the cost'. This popular expression comes closer to the views of spiritual teachers. Many of them suggest that it is 'through giving that we receive', though they would also say that to give with the specific purpose of receiving is not true giving.

Love is shown in caring, sharing and supporting. It is when you are personally most intact that you are most emotionally available to others and able to pay attention to their needs without your wants getting in the road.

Love is shown in caring, sharing and supporting. It is when you are personally most intact that you are most emotionally available to others and able to pay attention to their needs without your wants getting in the road. The capacity to express love is based on your wellbeing. As you grow in your capacity to love so you become more lovable, more in tune with reality and more in control of your life or, alternatively, less controlled by your wants, desires or the motives of others. A follower of Lao-tse would recognise, for example, that overweening ambition drives out love.

Close in meaning to love is *compassion*. You demonstrate this when you recognise the needs of others without being caught up in their emotional demands, desires or attachments. When you respond compassionately you do not, necessarily, give the other person what they want, but rather what they need. Mind you, being compassionate may not be something you can always do well.

To be truly compassionate in the Christian tradition you would probably need to be a saint or in the Buddhist tradition to have reached enlightenment! But don't worry, everyone is capable of learning to better understand others and their needs and so increasingly to act compassionately. This kind of learning will happen over time as you learn about yourself and others through paying attention to your feelings, thoughts and experiences. It will also be aided by following one of the practices, described later in this chapter, of prayer, meditation, or contemplation, whichever is best suited to your views.

Death

In Victorian times, sex was an absolutely taboo subject. These days it is often death that has become clandestine, sanitised and hidden. We do not discuss it much. While plenty of people are killed on television, either fictionally or actually, few people are familiar with the reality of death and dying.

In religious traditions, reminders of mortality have often been used to encourage a peaceful life of devotion. There is a story about an order of monks which used to require its members to make their own coffins, so that they faced the temporary nature of their existence ('remember man thou art but dust'), and in Tibetan Buddhism there is much emphasis on preparation for a good death. These teachings are not intended to make people despair, rather by fully understanding the nature of living (our connections with others; the specific opportunities offered by life), it is intended you will be better able to make the most of life and to appreciate the good things it offers— birds, trees, flowers, food, sex, sleep, sunshine and rain.

> If you view happiness as living solely to fulfil your every desire, then death is not something you will wish to contemplate. If, on the other hand, you see your happiness as bound up in the meaning of life and your contribution to it, then death is part of life and you may be content with that.

If you view happiness as living solely to fulfil your every desire, then death is not something you will wish to contemplate, since it is often considered to mean, as far as is known, the end of these opportunities. If, on the other hand, you see your happiness as bound up in the meaning of life and your contribution to it, then death is part of life and you may be content with that. Like Uncle Charlie you can enjoy things as they come along. Perhaps you already have, or see the potential to find, other meanings for living through a religious tradition, or it may be through your individual way of looking at the world, or because of some scientific understanding of life, or a combination of these explanations. There are many different ways of giving meaning to your life.

Near-death experiences may suggest evidence of life outside your body. Science has not been able to prove this though the near-death experience can be induced by the application of a drug.[16] However, it has been observed that near-death experiences are frequently followed by a change in the way a person sees life and in the way they subsequently live. Generally, people have a greater appreciation of the natural beauty of living and life's simpler pleasures. These changes are often accompanied by a more compassionate, supportive and appreciative relationship with others. People emerging from near-death experiences seem to live happier lives.

Celebrations

From ancient times, celebrations have been used to mark special occasions: births, marriages, harvests, initiations and deaths. Death in particular is celebrated when it is seen as transitory, or as a time to mark achievements. Celebrations are used in organised religions to help the adherents give meaning to their lives. In everyday life, too, there are occasions for celebration. There are New Year's Eve parties, anniversaries, and some holidays like Christmas, which were once primarily religious but are now less so.

Ceremonies and celebrations are a useful way to feel comfortable with yourself, to increase your recognition of your achievements, to encourage you to explore new vistas and give you a feeling of greater participation in living (control) rather than being a pawn of fate. In these ways, you can add further meaning to your life.

Although there are a range of celebrations or ceremonies that you enjoy, there are also a number of other opportunities which you may be missing. While, for example, twenty-first birthday parties are often held, there are few ceremonies or celebrations (other than those held in some religions) that formally mark the transition from adolescence to adulthood. This type of celebration can be enormously useful to parents, relatives, and the teenagers themselves. It adds meaning and improves confidence and expectations about the future. In a different context, a group of workers may have a celebration when the first prototype of a new car comes off the assembly line, or when a project is finished, or when the hospital team has successfully nursed their one-thousandth patient.

Exercise 23: Designing a ceremony to enter adulthood

You will need a couple of adults and at least one seventeen-year-old!

1. List a minimum of three changes or opportunities that will apply or become available on entering adulthood, e.g becoming eligible to vote. Some consequences may also arise from the particular family situation, such as becoming eligible to drive the family car, or do the ironing, or cook a pizza.
2. Design a way to show how each of these new opportunities/ responsibilities may be marked, e.g a test drive around the block to be viewed by family and friends; a specially presented new toy car; an ironing demonstration; a voucher for a home management course; giving, at a party, a speech on the responsibilities of adulthood delivered by the person, or a quiz on such responsibilities, and so on.

At the end of the ceremony, the teenager should have an increased understanding of what is required in their future role, know where to get the skills to perform these roles and feel supported by family and friends.

Prayer

FOR EXAMPLE

A friend of the family once asked a minister in his sixties what was the secret of his good skin; his response was 'prayer and sacrifice'. It is perhaps improbable, even from a religious point of view, that the results of prayer would be so direct!

While it remains common for people to pray for results of some kind—a successful marriage, a safe pregnancy, a pass in an examination or improved health, or a change in the weather—the more accepted religious view is to pray as a mark of respect or gratitude, and only to pray in a more general sense for results; perhaps for the happiness of others, or that your children will grow up to be 'good' people.

This latter view is more consistent with the notions expressed elsewhere in this book that trying to 'will' changes is not only likely to be unproductive in achieving happiness goals, but even counter-productive. So if you are someone who prays, try to focus on general changes (e.g. for peace and the wellbeing of others) rather than for specific results.

If you are not someone who prays, contemplation may provide you with feelings of comfort. To contemplate in this sense means to think about your life quietly and calmly, think about your associations with others and then try to develop attitudes which help you to live more in tune with your values. It could also mean mentally wishing others well. The Tibetan Buddhist tradition has a practice in which you mentally offer to take on board the troubles of another person and to offer them feelings of comfort and peace.

Meditation

The practice of meditation takes many forms. While there are forms of meditation in the Christian tradition, people usually refer to the practice developed by Eastern religions.

Meditation can be a spiritual exercise in that it seeks to help the practitioner detach from both the excitement as well as the worries of daily living and be more focused on the whole of life. Partly because of the way its practice encourages relaxation, it is seen as a way of improving your health and minimising stress on your immune system. There is evidence that shows meditation produces brainwave patterns that are different from the normal waking state. It may have far-reaching beneficial effects. In any case, its use has been widely reported as an adjunct in the treatment of cancer, sometimes as a method of increasing a person's feelings of calm and sometimes in imagining ways the body is helping itself to heal or contain the cancer.

There is little doubt that many people have found in meditation a way of improving their comfort and control in daily living. It is also possible that its regular use may increase creative capacities. Sometimes its practical effects may take a while to be noticed.

There have been many books written in recent years explaining how to meditate; several of these are referred to in Further Reading (page 239). Set out below are some suggestions on the practice of meditation, which include ideas that I have used for myself and with people I have counselled. The emphasis here is on getting started. Once you find you've begun to enjoy mediation, you may choose to study a particular form more closely.

Exercise 24: Practising meditation

Introduction

A number of options are provided within this exercise. You are advised to choose the set of options that seem to suit you best and to stick with them for at least a month. It is probable that with regular practice you will find that you are ready to add, amplify or to change your practice. It is best, however, that you do not change your practice simply because you feel you are not getting results. It is not wise to look for results. Just do the practice; preferably at the same time each day and in the same place, without comparing what happens on different days.

The setting

The kind of attitude you have can influence your meditation. Sometimes a spiritual attitude, or, if you prefer, an attitude that draws you into the spirit of the practice, can be encouraged by your surroundings. You may choose a particular room or a special corner of a room, perhaps with calming pictures, statues or fragrances. Garden settings may create a relaxing and harmonious atmosphere. The neat Japanese Zen garden with small plants, carefully arranged large stones, raked gravel and a small pond provides a visually calming scene for quite contemplation—often considered an ideal meditation site. The setting should also be free from the interruption of telephone calls and the needs of others.

Posture

You need to be sitting erect with your head, neck and spine in line. You know you probably have it 'right' when the back of your neck is touching your collar. Sitting in a cross-legged lotus position like a statue of Buddha, with the foot of one leg on the top of the knee of the other leg requires practice and nimble joints. You can sit in a simpler cross-legged position without being a contortionist. If you use either of these positions you will need to sit on a couple (or more) pillows or cushions, depending on your body weight. These days many Westerners practise meditation sitting in a chair without arms, but still using the erect head position and being careful not to lean on the back of the chair.

Many beginners find it is easiest to start practising with their eyes closed. In the Tibetan tradition, some practitioners begin with their head erect and eyes open and focused downwards, then they slowly raise their eyes in the first few seconds of practice until they are focused straight ahead. If you try this, you must look normally at something that is in your central vision, even if after a while you are not specifically aware of it. It is suggested that this form of practice prevents you from going to sleep!

Doing

In the Zen school of Buddhism, there is a meditation practice called Zazen, which simply means just sitting. Strictly speaking, meditation is not doing anything. It is just being aware, being conscious, without ruminating thoughts, planning or worrying. Theoretically you could just sit and be aware of the world and your presence in it. Rarely do people find this possible. Generally, you need to find an approach which will help you let go consciousness-demanding thoughts. Two common strategies are explored below.

Method 1

Mantras are a feature of the well-known practice of transcendental meditation (TM), which we can utilise. Adherents are personally given a mantra (a word, saying or expression) that they use in their meditation. Many mantras include words or sayings from other languages. You can use a word or expression which best suits you. It could be an everyday word like 'love', 'peace', 'calm', 'space' or 'emptiness', a religious expression, or if you prefer, an Eastern expression like 'Om manee padmay Om' (spelt phonetically), which roughly means 'Let a flower bloom in your heart'. With such expressions it is the resonance of the sound that is as important as the meaning. Some meditators even suggest learning by heart whole prayers and repeating them. When you use a word or expression you can repeat the word out aloud or in your head. Some words, like the famous 'om' also produce a sound which can resound within you helping you to be calm. Some forms of meditation ask the practitioner to hum aloud rather than say a mantra.

If you decide to use this method, you should choose a word and repeat it slowly under your breath or in your head with a feeling of reverence or appreciation. The word is repeated on the out-breath and the timing of the breathing is the same as described in the next method.

Method 2

The other common way to meditate is to do some form of breath counting. Assume your posture and then breathe out slowly while you count, say, up to three (initially), though you can increase it (to any number between three and ten) as you become more used to the method. Breathing should not to be forced or laboured, but natural and relaxed. Relaxed breathing is fairly slow; with slight natural pauses between breaths. Three breaths can take 13 to 15 seconds.

Initially, your meditation session should go for five to ten minutes. Choose a time and stick to it for a week—a longer time is not necessarily better. As you become more experienced in practice, you can increase the length of your practice, say to half an hour. You then may want to increase your sitting to twice a day.

Comments on meditation practice

It is common to have thoughts coming into your head, even after years of meditation practice. It is your attitude to them that is critical. Handle these outside thoughts in the same way you deal with worrying thoughts. Specifically, don't entertain them by inviting them to have a conversation with you, and don't fight them; just notice them, label them ('I am thinking ego-thoughts about how I am going to do that job' or 'That work is very important to me' or 'What is my partner going to say to me about last night?') then return to focusing on your breath counting, or saying your special word.

You may also feel minor discomforts such as an itchy nose, a body ache or an irritating fly. Deal with these feelings in the same way you handle unnecessary thoughts. Don't try to fight them, rather, refocus on your breath counting.

Sometimes you may notice physical changes while you meditate. A common one is a tingling sensation in the hands. The best thing to do with these feelings is to treat them like the distracting thoughts, that is, recognise their presence and then go back to your word, saying or breath counting—unless they are obviously distressing in which case meditation should be stopped.

Summary

You have learnt:

- about the role of blame, forgiveness and reparation in regaining or maintaining happiness.
- steps you can take to obtain forgiveness.
- the significance of the religious ideas of surrender (acceptance) and freedom in your life.
- how you can recognise many of life's teachings.

- how an appreciation of your place in the world and the meaning you give to living can help how you feel.
- how the kind of love you experience and give makes a difference.
- the connection of death with life and its role in happiness.
- the part played by celebrations and ceremonies in our lives and how ceremonies can be designed to suit our needs.
- the role of prayer.
- examples of meditation practices.

PART 3

PUTTING IT TOGETHER

Happiness revisited

The kind of happiness you are seeking is a personal matter though you will most likely have some goals common to others. In the first part of *Help Yourself to Happiness*, you selected goals under the broad headings of *comfort*, *control* and *creativity*. This allowed you to perceive happiness in real, practical and everyday situations. By now, you should really know that happiness means not only acquiring it, but also holding on to it, avoiding losing it, and, if for some reason it is lost, getting it back again.

All aspects of your life, have an impact on your happiness goals. Don't take a narrow focus. The meaning you give to living is crucial to your happiness. Search for happiness inside and outside of you by pursuing 'right' thinking (inside) and 'right' actions (outside).

Five pathways to happiness

Along with the eight principles that we have already explored, there are five key pathways to happiness. Each pathway is a living skill which will benefit you many times over once you have mastered it.

1. *Live in a relaxed and calm manner.* Manage your appetites, get a good night's sleep, manage stress and pain.
2. *Use more of your mind's abilities.* Improve your communication skills, learn new skills, work out how to change your ideas when necessary, and develop self-appreciation.
3. *Develop your in-built creative skills.* Give yourself wise advice. Maximise all your personal resources.
4. *Improve your capacity to relate effectively to others.* Establish effective and stable relationships. Care for others. Share your resources.
5. *Know how to minimise the harmful effects of loss.* Learn how to handle losses incurred through addictions, trauma experiences or death. While you cannot control many of these events, your happiness relies on your ability to control the damage and recover from the loss.

Exercise 25: Revising your goals

Return to the target goals you established in Exercise 2 (page 40) and review them in the light of the key pathways above and the eight happiness principles summarised on pages 46–56.

- What, if anything do you want to change?
- Why?
- What do you need to do to meet these new goals?
  Make a list.

Remember how to eat an elephant—take one bite at a time.

Seven happiness activities of a balanced life

Maintaining your joy in living means being ready to explore and play with the opportunities for learning that life offers.

A person whose life is balanced is best placed to leap aboard as opportunities arise.

Balanced happy lives usually feature a range of activities which are consistent with positive *comfort, control* and *creativity* happiness goals.

Relaxation and peace

In our pressure-cooker society you can feel stressed whatever your lifestyle. It is probable that you need to undertake steps to be more peaceful, calm and comfortable, if you aren't already doing that.

As well as the exercises suggested earlier—stomach breathing (page 89), progressive muscle relaxation (page 88), visualising and relaxing in your special place and meditation (page 93)—there are tapes on relaxation in most libraries. Relaxing forms of music, such as Pachelbel's Cannon in D, are extremely useful. Gardening, walking or just sitting watching the trees or the birds all promote a feeling of peace and contentment. Even pauses of just a few minutes during your day, when you simply notice what is happening inside you and around you, help remind you to be serene and unhurried.

Excitement

Excitement is an essential part of a balanced happy life. Being too laid-back can work against you. A small amount of stress promotes action and improves performance—performances with which you can be pleased, gratified and proud. There are plenty of images on which to draw: the picture of the artist, composer or writer moving about restlessly trying to get the inspiration to move on with their creation; the tension in the footballer or tennis player before the big match; the on-edge feeling before an examination, or the excitement of the family party you are

The irreverent Oscar Wilde used to say that the best way to get rid of temptation was to give into it. I suspect that it would be wise, however, to add to his statement, 'but not often or always!'

organising. Excitement is part of your natural condition. Whether it is part of your creative or control happiness goals depends on how you respond to it.

Excitement can even be seen as part of your comfort goals, insofar as a period of sensual excitement can lead us to a period of greater calm. The irreverent Oscar Wilde used to say that the best way to get rid of temptation was to give in to it. I suspect that it would be wise, however, to add to his statement, 'but not often or always!'

If stress is excessive then, not surprisingly, it causes distress. It is again a question of balance. Your ancient ancestors had the capacity to produce the emotional surges necessary for strong actions, but also the capacity to relax when the threat or challenge had passed. The problem is to avoid the continuance of the emotional response long after the event (e.g. worrying, or being angry, about those critical comments for two days).

Exercise and diet

You will probably be well aware of the general requirements for a healthy life. They usually include modest exercise three times a week for half an hour or more and a diet that includes the major food groups in recommended proportions. You probably know what to do, or where to go to get the right advice.

The main point in the present context is that you take the time to follow the available advice. To be successful may mean using a simple easy-to-follow routine rather than taking on complicated difficult-to-follow diets. It is probably easier to modify your lifestyle bit by bit. Work out a basic eating pattern that you don't have to think about too much, instead of spending your time counting calories before each meal. The same applies to exercise—a simple routine done with someone else to help 'keep you honest' is likely to be effective.

Living in moderation, in a balanced way, is more likely to improve happiness than life at either extreme—too much or too little. For instance, it is possible to exercise to the point of physical damage but it is certainly not a constructive thing to

do. Likewise, being a couch potato is hardly likely to be satisfying your happiness goals.

Appreciation and participation

Enjoying the creations of others is usually a pleasure, as is
participation in the arts. On some occasions your enjoyment
will be on a spiritual level, as well as the creative and instructive, especially when the piece of art, theatre, film or pop song
delivers a useful message on how to live.

Listening to music and songs, or watching a dance troupe
on stage or in a video clip, can be a source of happiness.
Indeed the mood and messages can range from expressions
of comfort, self-control and creativity to spiritual ones. Perhaps even more importantly and for the same reasons, personal participation in individual and group singing and
dancing can often lead you to your goals. The recently popular line dancing is similar in many ways to the group dancing
of both the nineteenth century and festive gatherings of our
much more distant ancestors. Dancing seems to address a
fairly basic need. Interpretive forms of dance, such as ballet,
continue to be popular as spectacles. Singing opportunities
abound, from formal chorale groups to amateur theatricals
and myriad paid and unpaid bands, as well as in churches and
homes.

Why don't you plan your time so that you can listen to and
watch music and dance, or, if possible, participate in or create it?
Someone once said that 'a stomach ulcer is an unwritten poem'.
While you may not want to write poetry, you can probably readily appreciate the sentiments expressed in this comment.

Moral, spiritual or religious activities

To live in harmony with yourself, others and the world,
requires you to be true to your values and to interact with others and with the larger environment in ways consistent with
their respective needs. To do otherwise is to foster discontent
and unhappiness.

This may mean active involvement with a church or religious tradition. Or it may mean adopting spiritual or moral attitudes, which, for example, stress the importance of helping others and avoiding damage to the environment and other human resources, as well as living in wonder at the beauty of the world and the universe.

One way of helping you to do this is to spend ten minutes each day reading an uplifting text. This could range from the bible to biographies of inspiring people, from books of sayings and quotes to stories of heroism, honesty, honour and love. Even the comic strips in daily newspapers may offer us human insight and moral understanding. Ten minutes of prayer, or contemplation, or just observing nature may similarly be helpful. The important thing is to do it every day if you possibly can.

Productivity

The story goes that when Freud was asked what happiness was he replied with just three words 'love and work'. Being productive is generally part of everyone's 'reason for being' and therefore part of your happiness.

For productivity to be seen as constructive, you need to recognise its presence and its possibilities. Even in a nursing home, unless mentally disabled, a person can be productive according to the level of their physical capacity (e.g. spending time with less able residents; being available to be asked questions about the past by small groups of children; asking questions of and listening supportively to family visitors; reading and summarising information for others, and so on). You can be productive whatever your circumstances.

Whatever your occupation, if you see what you are doing as useful to others or yourself, you are on the right road to happiness.

Relationships

Even though solitude is a legitimate and often a positive choice, for many people having a good relationship with a partner is important. What you say and do and what others do (though you cannot control them) matters.

You are most likely to implement the relationship supportive activities canvassed in this book when you are able to take into consideration the needs of others. To learn to appreciate others and to form new supportive relationships often requires new social opportunities such as joining a club or group, or taking a recreational or further education course. You just have to take the first step. And you are most likely to be able to do that when you have calmed your own desires and have taken quite deliberate steps to set aside time (even just once a week) to observe others and reflect on their needs.

What now?

Given the wide range of possible steps you could take towards your happiness goals, you may want to know where to start! It is useful to have a base plan to which you can return, say, every six months to see how you are going and what new targets you may need to address.

The next exercise below is designed to do this. It assumes that there are aspects of your life that you want to change in pursuit of your happiness goals.

Exercise 26: Planning changes

Record the answers to the questions that follow. Your answers and notes should take up no more than one A4 page.

What do you want to change?
Choose a change you would like to achieve—one that belongs to your *comfort, control* or *creativity* goals. Your choice needs to be:

Realistic—something you could expect to achieve with reasonable effort.

Participatory—it needs to involve an action on your part, not simply a wish that something will change. It may be changing the way you think about something—you could decide to appreciate yourself more.

Noticeable—you need to have some way of noticing or measuring the expected change.

For example, you have decided to become calmer. How will you notice your success? Look for the following indicators of change:

- feeling calmer during meetings;
- sleeping better;
- fewer arguments;
- feeling more relaxed while driving;
- better concentration when reading or watching television;
- less restless and so on.

Other change goals can similarly be broken down into a number of indicators that show that the goal is being reached.

What do you want to achieve?

Once you have chosen your goal, you then need to see whether it is your understanding, your feelings or your skills that you are seeking to change. If you have decided you want to become more relaxed then is it because you hope to understand your partner better when you are in a relaxed frame of mind, or do you want to access peaceful feelings, or improve your skills in managing your distressing unreasonable thoughts? Alternatively, you may simply want to play darts, bridge or bowls better, or improve your swimming style, your cooking or computer skills, and know that you'll be able to do this if you are more relaxed and receptive.

How will you do this?

What steps will you need to take to achieve the change? This may already be clear to you. If not, check the list of exercises on page 11, or you may have an idea from some other source. Decide what information and resources you will need (e.g. tapes, paper, other people), the steps you will need to take, the order in which you will take them, the time you will need and if you need a place to practise. Be specific!

What could hinder you?

Take into account other factors. These may be family chores or responsibilities, work commitments or personal circumstances (e.g. an illness). Make suitable arrangements in advance to ensure that these factors do not interfere with your plan.

It has been said that the best time to give up smoking is when you are out alone on a fortnight's camp!

Should something prevent you from pursuing your target goal it would be better to choose another activity that could more easily be achieved, rather than do nothing.

How will you know when you have achieved your goal?

To know if you have been successful you need to have described in advance a number of bench-markers. What can be seen in yourself or your circumstances that can be recognised as change?

Remember that some of the issues we are talking about are lifestyle changes and you should look for continued progression rather than an immediately obvious specifiable outcome. Meditation practice is one example where change is often gradual.

Having a supporter

It is useful to have a trusted friend (who may or may not be a partner) with whom you can share your plans, from whom you can accept constructive comments and who can help you judge if you have succeeded, or are succeeding. He or she will be someone whom you consult at the beginning to see if your plans seem reasonable, as you go along, to see that things are on the right track, and when you think you have reached your particular goal, to check it out and note your achievement. Eastern religions refer to gurus or teachers to serve this purpose, while Christians have historically used priests, pastors and ministers. In the business world in America, trainers use a buddy system to support new learners. Whatever way you look at it, having a key supporter can be very helpful to you in your pursuit of change. Think about it now. Who can perform this role for you?

Use the 'What now?' format to plan successive changes. It may sometimes be possible to draw up a plan for a couple of changes concurrently.

If all this seems like a bit of work, it is worth remembering that if you really want to be happier, change is necessary, and that means doing something different from what you already do.

Some final words

Thinking about the meaning of happiness reminds me of the riddles I heard as a child. They had a pattern. 'I am not in so-and-so, but I am in such-and-such. What am I?' What is the answer to the happiness riddle? Happiness is not wealth which, despite all the media messages, is happiness neutral. Money, whether quickly obtained, inherited or gradually accumulated may help, but it can hinder. This is good in a way because it means you can seek happiness in other pursuits, for which, in some cases, income may be a by-product. Happiness exists in living effectively with, and handling, the inevitable ups and downs of life, which happen to us all. It is in humour, in not taking ourselves too seriously, and in love in all its expressions. It is about developing our self-control rather than in controlling others.

For some people happiness is a misleading goal, when it is thought to imply the restless pursuit of, often, non-satisfying pleasure. However, in this book 'the pleasure principle' has not been a happiness principle. The kind of happiness that is most likely to be enduring and fulfilling is better described as 'joy'.

Although you probably have immediate *comfort*, *control* and *creativity* goals, development is continuous practice, learning and growth. I hope that you have found some personal next steps. I am working on mine!

NOTES

[1]In the highly acclaimed manual, Constructing the Sexual Crucible, W. W. Norton, New York, 1991, David Schnarch amongst a wealth of clinical detail about sexuality, intimacy and eroticism makes the point that effective interpersonal relationships form the basis for developing an ongoing and satisfying intimate one.

[2]D. M. Warburton, 'Pleasure is good for you', vol. 49, no 1, *IPA Review*, pp. 24–28, 1996.

[3]Douglas Davis, *The Five Myths of Television Power or Why the Medium Is Not the Message*, Simon and Schuster, New York, 1993, p. 15.

[4]Based on an idea suggested in *Kinds of Minds—Towards an Understanding of Consciousness*, Daniel C. Dennett, HarperCollins, London 1996.

[5]Zdenek, Marilee, *The Right-Brain Experience*, Corgi, Great Britain, 1983. She discusses, amongst other things, various ways of using the 'wrong' side of our body to release creative resources.

[6]Zohar, Danah, *The Quantum Self*, Flamingo HarperCollins, London, 1991, p. 104.

[7]National Statistics website: www.statistics.gov.uk (Crown copyright material is reproduced with the permission of the Controller of HMSO).

[8]Leon Earle—research work on retired men, appearing in *Successful Ageing in Australian Society*, Community Development Project, Recreation for Older Adults (ROA), Canberra, 1996. This work has focused on men's need for sheds in which to engage in some independent productive activity. I have expanded this view to include

women, as it seems reasonable to suggest that women also benefit from some form of independent productive activity.

[9]Richard Chasin, Henry Grunebaum and Margaret Herzig (eds), *One Couple Four Realities: Multiple Perspectives on Couple Therapy*, The Guilford Press, New York, 1990.

[10]Phyllis Silverman of Harvard Medical School discussed her ideas with Geraldine Doogue on *Compass* ABC TV 7 June 1998.

[11]Lyndon Walker, 'Melanie Klein's Concept of Reparation and its Use in the Counselling of Clients Who Have Suffered Significant Abuse in Their Past', a paper presented at the Australian Family Therapy Conference, Adelaide, 1997.

[12]C. S. Nott, *Teachings of Gurdjieff*, Routledge and Kegan Paul, London, 1961.

[13]Lin Yutang (translator), *The Wisdom of Lao-tse* Random House, New York, 1948.

[14]Victor Frankl, a psychiatrist and a Jew who spent some time in a Nazi concentration camp argued that survival in these terrible circumstances was more likely if the person could give some meaning to living. The school of therapy he founded is known as logotherapy, or meaning therapy. *Man's Search For Meaning*, Victor E. Frankl, 3rd edition, Simon and Schuster Inc., New York, 1984.

[15]Stuart Kauffman, *At Home in the Universe: the Search for the Laws of Complexity*, Penguin, London, 1996.

[16]Karl L.R. Jansen, 'Using Ketamine to Induce the Near-Death Experience' in *Jahrbuch f. Ethnomedizin*, Berlin, 1995, pp. 55–79

FURTHER READING

These titles are listed in order of the development of topics in the book. Except for the first two information books on TV, the remainder are focused on self-help ways of improving an aspect of your life.

Silvertone, Roger, *Television and Everyday Life*, Routledge, London, 1994

Davis, Douglas, *The Five Myths of Television Power or Why the Medium Is Not the Message*, Simon & Schuster, New York, 1993

Weisbluth, Marc *Sleep Well: Peaceful Nights for You and Your Child*, Unwin Hymon, London, 1987

Rose, Leonard, *Overcoming Pain*, McCulloch, Victoria, 1990

Shone, Ronald, *Creative Visualization*, HarperCollins, Aquarian Press edition, London, 1993

Fanning, Patrick, *Visualization For Change*, New Harbinger, Oakland, USA, 1988

Zdenek, Marilee, *The Right-Brain Experience*, Corgi, London, 1983

Houston, Jean, *The Possible Human: A Course in Enhancing Your Physical, Mental, and Creative Abilities*, J.P.Tarcher, Inc., California, 1982

Anderson, Jane, *Sleep On It*, Angus & Robertson, Sydney, 1994

O'Connor, Peter, *Dreams and the Search for Meaning*, Methuen, Victoria, 1986

Gray, John, *Men Are From Mars, Women Are From Venus* HarperCollins, London, 1992

Dowrick, Stephanie, *The Intimacy & Solitude Self-Therapy Book* Mandarin, 1993

Johnson, Kendall, *Turning Yourself Around: Self-Help for Troubled Teens*, Hunter House Inc., USA, 1992

Weinhold, Barry K. and Weinhold Janae B., *Breaking Free of the Co-Dependency Trap*, Stillpoint Publishing, Walpole, 1989

Watts, Rod and de L Horne, David J., *Coping With Trauma: The Victim and The Helper*, Australian Academic Press, Brisbane, 1994

Kübler-Ross, Elisabeth, *Living with Death and Dying*, Macmillan, USA, 1981

Fisher, Bruce, *Rebuilding When Your Relationship Ends*, Impact Publishers, 2nd ed, California, 1992

Seligman, Martin E.P., *What You Can Change & What You Can't*, Alfred A Knopf, New York, 1993

Borysenko, Joan, *Fire In the Soul*, Time Warner, New York, 1993

Beck, Charlotte Joko, *Nothing Special: Living Zen*, HarperCollins, New York, 1994

Fontana, David, *The Elements of Meditation*, Element Books, Rockport, USA, 1991

LeShan, Lawrence, *How To Meditate: A Guide to Self-discovery*, Bantam, New York, 1986

Campbell, Andrea, *Your Corner of the Universe: A Guide to Self-therapy Through Journal Writing*, Bob Adams, Inc., Massachusetts, 1993